新SAT

阅读真经总纲

刘洪波 编著

中国人民大学出版社
·北京·

推荐序

SAT 由美国大学委员会 (College Board) 主办，ETS 负责出题和阅卷，是目前世界上比较权威的能力测试。SAT 成绩是世界各国高中生申请美国大学入学资格及奖学金的重要参考。在 2016 年改革后，新 SAT 总分共 1 600 分，分为阅读、文法和数学三部分，写作改为选考。其成绩有效期为 2 年。

从整个考试结构来看，阅读能力在 SAT 考试中起着举足轻重的作用。本书旨在帮助考生提高阅读能力，使其不仅在 SAT 阅读考试中取得高分，而且能够提高对其他部分考试题目的阅读能力。全书包括七章，从题型和题材等不同角度进行考前训练。第一章主要分析 SAT 阅读考试的评分标准及测试要点。第二章至第四章按照题型讲解。信息与观点类题目包括词义题、细读题、关系题、引证题、中心题和总结题。修辞题分为分析选词题、分析目的题、分析论点题、分析态度题和分析结构题。综合题涉及分析多文本题和分析数据信息题。就题材而言，SAT 阅读涵盖文学类、历史社会类和科技类文章等类型。通过本书的讲解，读者可以充分了解 SAT 阅读的应试方法及主要考试内容。

本书由中国英语教学领军人物刘洪波老师执笔，站在提高英语能力、以实力夺取高分的角度全方位讲解。刘洪波老师是真经派创始人，洞悉中西方考试差异，旨在通过真经体系，搭建中国考生顺利实现海外留学的桥梁。在整个真经体系中，总纲侧重技法，真经注重实践，考点词专门夯实基础。

在本书出版之际，谨以此文代序，愿更多的考生取得好成绩，实现求学梦想。

吕蕾微信公众号：lvlei 1973

吕蕾微博地址：http://weibo.com/lvlei1973

一直播：76304044

目　录

第一章

洞察SAT阅读考试

亲爱的同学，你好呀！

在带领你学习SAT阅读真经之前，我先照例叮嘱几句。

我为学为贵集团编写的托福真经、雅思真经系列课堂使用教材，包括这本SAT真经，都有以下几个特点：

★ **文字语言比较轻松俏皮**（因为备考学习本就很累，怕你读不下去）；

★ **原创的技巧方法很多**（可能颠覆你以前的认知，请不要怀疑，大胆试用吧）；

★ **字越少事越大**（重要技巧表述很精炼易于记忆，彩色字体是在敲黑板、划重点！）。

好啦，就这些，Let's stuck in!

读者福利：扫码免费学习《SAT 阅读入门真经第一课》

一、SAT 阅读考试形式

首先，大家来了解一下 SAT 考试构成：

SAT (Scholastic Assessment Test)		
考试内容	考试时间（分钟）	题目数量
Reading	65	52
Writing and Language	35	44
Math	80	58
Essay (optional)	50	1
Total	**180 (230 with Essay)**	**154 (155 with Essay)**

- 如上图所示，SAT考试分为四个部分，其中第四部分Essay（短文写作）是选考。

- Reading（阅读）是考试的第一部分，要求65分钟完成52道题，平均每道题花1分15秒。

接下来，我们看看 SAT 阅读考试具体的形式：

SAT阅读			
五篇文章	内容	主题	题目数量
一篇	小说节选，来自美国文学或世界文学	文学	10
一篇或双短文	美国建国文献或国际知名演讲、信件节选	历史与社会研究	21
一篇	社会科学类文章，比如：经济学、心理学、社会学		

两篇或一篇加双短文	科学领域文章，比如：地球科学、生物、化学、物理	科学	21

- 由五篇文章构成（*四篇文章加一篇双短文*），分别对应*文学、历史与社会研究、科学*三大主题。

- 每篇文章长度为500～750词，五篇文章共3 250词左右。

- 五篇文章中会有一篇实际上包含两篇比较短的小文章（双短文），考生需要在问题之中对这两篇短文进行对比和比较。

- 考生需要对*两个*与文章相关的*图表*进行分析。

- 文章难度介于高中初级和大学初级水平之间。

- 总共52个A、B、C、D单选题，*答错题不会被扣分（不能空，不会就蒙）*！

最后，我们了解一下分数换算。

- SAT考试总分1 600分，其中Math（数学）800分，Evidence-Based Reading and Writing（循证阅读和写作）800分。

- 在Evidence-Based Reading and Writing（循证阅读和写作）中，Reading（阅读）占400分，Writing and Language（写作和语言）占400分。

- 新SAT考试正式的分数报告很全面，会从多个维度分析。同时分数换算比较复杂，每次考试成绩都会经过曲度处理，即一个固定分值所对应的答对问题数量视考试当日的情况而定。下面提供一个简易对照表供大致参考：

新SAT阅读考试分数对应表			
正确题数	对应分数	正确题数	对应分数
52	400	40	330
51	400	39	320
50	390	38	320
49	380	37	310
48	380	36	310
47	370	35	300
46	370	34	300
45	360	33	290
44	350	32	290
43	350	31	280
42	340	30	280
41	330		

二、SAT 阅读考查技能

★ 考试目的

官方申明：SAT 阅读考查你是否能理解各种类型的文章，包括文学类（literary）和信息类（informational）文章，而这些文章很可能是你将来在大学和职场上会碰到的。

☆ 考查技能

官方申明：在阅读中强调两大技能：Command of Evidence（对证据的掌控）和 Words in Context（语境中的词义）。

考生将来在大学和职场上，经常会使用诸如细节（details）、例子（examples）、理由（reasons）、事实（facts）、数据（figures）等证据，去支持自己的观点或驳斥别人的观点。

这正是 SAT 阅读考试设计测试的重点，同时 SAT 官方希望，通过这些阅读考题的练习，能潜移默化地培养考生的逻辑性思维和准确有效的交流能力。

Command of Evidence（对证据的掌控）能力测试体现在 SAT 阅读考试中，包含四个方面：

方面1： 寻找某一问题在文章中最有力的证据（理解*细节*）

方面2： 理解全文中心思想（理解*大意*）

方面3： 理解作者的论证手法（理解*手法*）

方面4： 理解数据图表信息，并得出数据和文本信息之间的关系（理解*数据*）

Words in Context（语境中的词义）能力测试体现在 SAT 阅读考试中，包含两个方面：

方面1： 理解上下文中词义和表达（理解*细节*）

方面2： 分析词汇选择的修辞目的（理解*手法*）

三、SAT 阅读题型分类

虽然 SAT 所有阅读题都是 A、B、C、D 单选题，看上去形式一致，但实际上每道题的测试考点和命题目的是不同的。

根据《最新 SAT 考试官方指南》，52 道阅读题可分为*三大类，共 13 种*。

⭐ 信息与观点题（*Information and Ideas*）

这类题目对应了 Command of Evidence 中第 1 点、第 2 点，以及 Words in Context 中第 1 点。考查考生对文章内容含义的理解。包含了从考查单词理解，到句子、上下文关系，再到段落中心和全文中心，共六种，十分全面。

(1) 词义题（Interpreting Words and Phrases in Context）

(2) 细读题（Reading Closely）

(3) 引证题（Citing Textual Evidence）

(4) 中心题（Determining Central Ideas and Themes）

(5) 总结题（Summarizing）

(6) 关系题（Understanding Relationships）

⭐ 修辞题（*Rhetoric*）

修辞题对应了 Command of Evidence 中第 3 点和 Words in Context 中第 2 点的能力测试。这类题不再是考查考生对文章本身内容意思（What）的理解，而是更深入、更高级了，考查对作者的论证手法、写作手法、行文目的、选词偏好的理解，也就是考查 How。

修辞题细分为以下 5 种：

(7) 分析选词题（Analyzing Word Choice）

(8) 分析目的题（Analyzing Purpose）

(9) 分析态度题（Analyzing Point of View）

(10) 分析论点题（Analyzing Arguments）

(11) 分析结构题（Analyzing Text Structure）

★ 综合题（Syntheses）

顾名思义，综合题就是考查对两处信息的合并理解。对数据和文本的合并理解对应了 Command of Evidence 中第 4 点能力；对双短文中的信息合并理解则对应了 Command of Evidence 中第 1 点和第 2 点能力。

所以综合题分为下面两种题型：

（12）分析多文本题（Analyzing Multiple Texts）

（13）分析数据信息题（Analyzing Quantitative Information）

以上三大类共 13 种题型的解题技巧真经将在第二章、第三章、第四章详细逐一讲解。请务必认真学习掌握。

四、SAT 阅读特色及备考应对

很多考生在备考 SAT 的同时，也在准备托福、雅思等英语语言考试。和托福、雅思阅读相比，SAT 阅读有以下九大特色，相应的，应试方法也有以下九个重大不同：

★ SAT 文章体裁多样

SAT 阅读考试的五篇文章中，小说节选和文件演讲稿的文章体裁是托福、雅思阅读考试中没有的。很多考生对这两种体裁不熟悉，刚接触会感觉非常不适应，必须要花额外时间进行针对性阅读训练。

★ SAT 文章较短

托福、雅思阅读考试文章每篇长 1 000 词左右，而 SAT 阅读文章每篇长 500 ～ 750 词。所以，SAT 阅读更适合先通读全文，然后再做题。

★ SAT 题目定位简单

与托福雅思阅读题目相比，SAT 题目的定位通常更清晰、更简单。基于这个特点，

SAT 阅读可以*先通读全文，然后再做题*；而托福、雅思阅读则应该是先读题，对题目有了印象，再读文章，帮助题目定位。

★ *SAT* 中心思想题权重大

与托福、雅思阅读的题目相比，SAT 阅读中考查段落中心、全文中心、自然段关系、全文结构的题目更多。所以，SAT 更强调对文章宏观层面的理解，**更应该*先通读全文，然后再做题*。**

★ *SAT* 修辞题权重大

托福阅读也考查修辞题，但权重小；雅思阅读基本不考修辞；而 SAT 阅读中修辞题是重要考试内容。所以 SAT 要求对文章有更精致、更深入的理解，因此**更适合*先通读全文，然后再做题*。**

★ *SAT* 独特的引证题

SAT 独有，托福、雅思不考。大多数情况下问前一题答案的原文证据，用来考查你是否真的找到了前一道题的原文出处和证据，而不是靠运气蒙对了答案。该题型解题技巧参考本书第二章。

★ *SAT* 独特的数据图

SAT 独有，托福、雅思不考。考查对图表中数据含义的理解和规律的总结。因为图表样式繁杂、图中数据多，乍一看很吓人，其实但凡拥有常规读图能力的考生，再注意几个要点，都能轻松拿分。该题型解题技巧参考本书第四章。

★ *SAT* 独特的双短文

SAT 独有，托福、雅思不考。乍一看很难，要读两篇短文，其实这两篇短文加起来一共也就 700 词左右，相当于一篇 SAT 长篇文章。注意这两篇短文各自的中心大意，搞定两者之间的关系即可。该题型解题技巧参考本书第四章。

☆ *SAT* 独特的综合题

托福其实也有综合命题概念。比如托福综合写作题，要求考生先读一篇短文，再听一位教授对该话题的观点评论，最后综合上述的阅读和听力内容，写一篇文章。

与托福不同，SAT阅读要求综合图表数据和文本信息，或者综合双短文信息来答题。该题型解题技巧参考本书第四章。

第二章

信息与观点题
（Information and Ideas）
技巧真经

信息与观点题考查对文章内容信息的理解。

这类题目涵盖了从对具体单词、数据、句子的命题，到抽象的段落中心和全文中心思想的考查。

SAT 阅读要求考生能同时理解作者通过文字直接传递的信息观点和间接暗示的信息观点。

信息与观点题是很多英语阅读考试中的常规设计，比如在托福、雅思等阅读考试中，主要考查这类题目，所以，考生对这类题目应该并不陌生。

在 SAT 阅读中，信息与观点题细分为以下六类。

一、词义题（Interpreting Words and Phrases in Context）

二、细读题（Reading Closely）

三、关系题（Understanding Relationships）

四、引证题（Citing Textual Evidence）

五、中心题（Determining Central Ideas and Themes）

六、总结题（Summarizing）

一、词义题（Interpreting Words and Phrases in Context）

词义题要求选出单词在原文中的精确含义（the precise meaning），重点考查上下文语境理解。

题干标志词：most nearly means。

出题频率：高。

★ 题目形式

> **Question**
>
> As it is used in line 54, "convey" most nearly means
>
> A) transport.
>
> B) counteract.
>
> C) exchange.
>
> D) communicate.

★ 技巧真经

1. 不是找同义词选项

被考查单词很可能是多义词，很可能四个选项都是它的同义词；一定要回原文阅读，理解其在文中所使用的特定词义。

2. 不能只读一句话

理解上下文的意思就是至少要读该句、它的上一句和下一句，共三句话。如果还理解不了，可以读整个自然段，甚至通过全文中心去判断。

3. 理解相邻句子间逻辑关系

句子之间是一定有关系的。捋清关系，可以通过读得懂的句子去猜测难句的大意。

4. 词本无义，义由境生

碰到被考查的单词不认识时，也不用惊慌，请默念该口诀定神。可将四个选项分别代入原文，选择最佳词义。

BTW (by the way)，平时积累、提升词汇量当然是必要的，同时，记单词的时候，要对一词多义重视起来。如何轻松记忆多义词？赠送一个 Free 彩蛋，扫码即可收听我的一个音频示例讲解。

二、细读题（Reading Closely）

细读题考查对文中一个观点或一个细节的理解，多要求对一句话或相邻几句话仔细阅读。这种题型还可具体分为明示题和暗示题，SAT 命题官方用两组单词来区分特点：direct（直接的）Vs. indirect（间接的），或者 explicit（直白的）Vs. implicit（含蓄的）。下面分别讲解。

A. 明示题

显然这种题型较简单，正确选项是对原文直接的、直白的转述改写。

题干标志词：According to the passage，states（说明），indicates（表明）等。

出题频率：高。

★ 题目形式

> **Question 43**
>
> The author of Passage 1 indicates that space mining could have which positive effect?
>
> A) It could yield materials important to Earth's economy.
>
> B) It could raise the value of some precious metals on Earth.
>
> C) It could create unanticipated technological innovations.
>
> D) It could change scientists' understanding of space resources.

★ 技巧真经

1. 准确快速定位原文

不同于词义题，这种题型的题干中通常没有说明出自原文哪一行，所以需要仔细阅读题干，画出 keywords，帮助快速定位原文出处。

比如本题，就需要画出 space mining 和 positive effect，回原文找到讲 positive effect 的地方。

2. 连连看，找多组同义替换

既然正确选项是原文的直接转述，那么正确选项中重要单词必然在原文中能找出它们的同义替换。我常说："高手和低手的区别，是他们看懂原文和答案之间的同义词的组数不同。"高手能找到正确选项中所有单词在原文中的同义词，会有一种明察秋毫的感觉（可参考本书第七章第 43 题的解析体会）。

3. 考查干扰选项

干扰选项的设计常用三个手法：驳斥原文、原文未提、答非所问。

当我们选出正确选项之后，再去快速浏览干扰选项，可以起到交叉检验的目的。

如果我们不能百分之百确认正确选项，浏览其他选项可以起到用排除法做题的目的。

BTW，牢记正确选项的特征：出现了和原文多组多义词替换。

B. 暗示题

这种题型出现概率小，一套题里有两个左右。正确选项是基于（based on）原文信息的合理的逻辑推导，或者说是话外之义、弦外之音。

题干标志词：Based on the passage，implies（暗示），it can reasonably（合理地）be inferred（推论）等。

出题概率：中。

★ 题目形式

Question 26

Based on the passage, the authors' statement "If a pair consisted of two purines, for example, there would not be room for it" (lines 29–30) implies that a pair

A) of purines would be larger than the space between a sugar and a phosphate group.

B) of purines would be larger than a pair consisting of a purine and a pyrimidine.

C) of pyrimidines would be larger than a pair of purines.

D) consisting of a purine and a pyrimidine would be larger than a pair of pyrimidines.

★ 技巧真经

1. 准确快速定位原文

同样地，暗示题也可能在题干中没有指明原文出处，需要画出 keywords 定位。

2. 阅读上下文，理解话外音

首先，要理解作者的话外音，必须要理解这句话出现的语境。所以扩展上下文阅读很重要。

其次，很多"贵粉儿"问：SAT 怎样考查 imply 和 infer？什么叫"合理的"推论？逻辑推导到哪一个深度层级合适？

只要牢记下面两个例子，你就能理解 SAT 的暗示题命题思路和难度了。

> 原文：A > B，B > C。暗示：**A > C**。
>
> 原文：在沙漠里，水比黄金更珍贵。暗示：*一种物资的价值不是绝对的，取决于环境场景。*

3. 考查干扰选项

同理，快速考查其他选项是有必要的。

BTW，正确选项中可能也会出现少量同义替换，但同义替换不是这种题的考点，不能作为选择的核心证据。

三、关系题（Understanding Relationships）

关系题考查文章中观点、人物、事件、信息等之间的关系理解，三大考查关系分别是：

因果（Cause-and-effect），题干标志词：because，since，why 等。

对比（Comparison-contrast），题干标志词：more，less 等。

顺序（Sequence），题干标志词：first，last，before，after 等。

出题概率：中。

★ 题目形式

Question

The authors indicate that people value gift-giving because they feel it

A) functions as a form of self-expression.

B) is an inexpensive way to show appreciation.

C) requires the gift-recipient to reciprocate.

D) can serve to strengthen a relationship.

★ 技巧真经

关系题的解题技巧和前面讲解的细读题的解题技巧一致。

唯一的区别是：要重视题干中的关系信号词，它本身就是用于定位的 keywords，也是重要解题线索。

例如，题干中问 why，回原文一定要找到因果关系。原文中可能没有 why 这个词，而可能是 therefore，thus，in order to，explanation，reason，affect 等任何一个表达因果关系的同义词（组）。

BTW，关系题其实是更简单的细读题。注意也有明示和暗示两种变化。

四、引证题（Citing Textual Evidence）

引证题是 SAT 阅读中的特色题型，大多数情况下紧跟在某一细读题后面出现，用来考查你是否真的找到了前一道题的原文出处和证据，而不是蒙对的答案。

题干标志：Which choice provides the best evidence for the answer to the previous question?

出题概率：高。

⭐ 题目形式

Question 4

Which reaction does Akira most fear from Chie?

A) She will consider his proposal inappropriate.

B) She will mistake his earnestness for immaturity.

C) She will consider his unscheduled visit an imposition.

D) She will underestimate the sincerity of his emotions.

Question 5

Which choice provides the best evidence for the answer to the previous question?

A) Line 33 ("His voice... refined")

B) Lines 49–51 ("You... mind")

C) Lines 63–64 ("Please... proposal")

D) Lines 71–72 ("Eager... face")

⭐ 技巧真经

1. 如前一题容易定位且简单，后面的引证题就是顺带送分

可以用引证题的正确选项来验证前一题的定位是否准确。

2. 如前一题难定位，可用后面引证题的四个选项去一一定位阅读，用排除法解前一题

引证题的四个选项相当于告诉你：原文这四处中有一处是上一题的命题出处，你不用浪费时间在全文中乱找。

BTW，引证题"出镜率"高，要完全掌握，并充分利用它拿分。因为它经常和前一题组队出现，一对就对两个，一错也错两个。

引证题偶尔也化装成"单身狗"，独自出现，形式如下：

Question 23

A student claims that nitrogenous bases pair randomly with one another. Which of the following statements in the passage contradicts the student's claim?

A) Lines 5–6 ("To each... types")

B) Lines 9–10 ("So far... irregular")

C) Lines 23–25 ("The bases... other")

D) Lines 27–29 ("One member... chains")

五、中心题（Determining Central Ideas and Themes）

中心题考查全文中心主旨或某自然段中心思想。下面分别讲解。

A. 全文中心题

题干标志词：theme（主题、主旨）of the passage。

出题概率：极低。

★ 题目形式

Question 1

Which choice best describes a major theme of the passage?

A) The corrupting influence of a materialistic society.

B) The moral purity of young children.

C) The bittersweet brevity of childhood naivete.

D) The restorative power of parental love.

★ 技巧真经

1. 中心题最后做

当做完其他题目后，考生对文章会加深理解，这对正确选择中心思想有极大帮助。

2. 如何寻找全文中心

有的文章有明显的全文中心句，多出现在首段、第二段和末段中，要重点阅读。

有的文章虽无明显中心句，但有某些 keywords 遍布全文，反复出现。找出来，画下来，看看哪个选项有同义词对应。

3. 理解选项中抽象单词

既然是提炼总结中心，就经常是考查正确选项中抽象词汇的理解，它们是对原文具体词汇和表达的同义归纳总结。

4. 避免以偏概全

中心题的干扰选项最常见的设计是：选项内容符合原文表达，是原文的具体信息或某个分论点，但不是全文中心。

BTW，虽然选全文中心的题目"出镜率"极低，但该题型对应的解题技巧极其重要，后面讲解的总结题以及下一章的分析态度题、分析论点题、分析结构题等均可通用，一定要掌握。

B. 段落中心题

题干标志词：main idea，main point，central idea of a paragraph。

出题概率：低。

☆ 题目形式

Question 18

The main idea of the final paragraph is that

A) Human quirks make it difficult to predict people's ethical decisions accurately.

B) People universally react with disgust when faced with economic injustice.

C) Understanding human psychology may help to define ethics in economics.

D) Economists themselves will be responsible for reforming the free market.

☆ 技巧真经

1. 找出段落中心句

分析段落内部句子之间的逻辑关系，重点阅读首句、第二句和末句。

2. 考查段落间逻辑

注意本段和上一段、下一段的段间逻辑关系。

3. 注意同义替换

理解正确选项中单词在段落中的同义词复现。

六、总结题（Summarizing）

总结题极其类似于全文中心题。细微的区别是：中心总结更简洁，而 summary（摘要）信息更丰富一点。

题干标志词：summarizes, summary。

出题概率：极低。

★ 题目形式

Question 1

Which choice best summarizes the passage?

A) A woman weighs the positive and negative aspects of accepting a new job.

B) A woman does not correct a stranger who mistakes her for someone else.

C) A woman impersonates someone else to seek revenge on an acquaintance.

D) A woman takes an immediate dislike to her new employer.

★ 技巧真经

与全文中心题技巧一致。

第三章

修辞题（Rhetoric）技巧真经

"修"，指修饰；"辞"，指语言。"修辞"，就是指说话的方式、手段。

修辞的概念可以追溯到古希腊的亚里士多德（Aristotle），他写了一本书叫《修辞学》，来阐述演讲的技巧，如何让你的语言更有感染力、说服力，更有力量。

在 SAT 阅读考试中，上一章学习的信息与观点题，强调的是理解作者通过文章传递的信息和观点（message），而本章的修辞题则强调理解文章作者的写作手法（craft）。

比如都是考单词，信息与观点题考查单词的词义（meaning）；而修辞题则考查作者为什么用这个词，作者用这个词的目的（purpose）。

或者我们可以这样理解，前者考 What，后者考 **How**。

在 SAT 阅读中，修辞题细分为以下五类。

一、分析选词题（Analyzing Word Choice）

二、分析目的题（Analyzing Purpose）

三、分析论点题（Analyzing Arguments）

四、分析态度题（Analyzing Point of View）

五、分析结构题（Analyzing Text Structure）

一、分析选词题（Analyzing Word Choice）

与上一章讲解的词义题不同，分析选词题考查考生去理解作者为什么使用这些词，这些词对文章的含义、风格、语气、感情色彩有什么作用和影响。

题干标志词：use the words, mainly to。

出题频率：中。

★ 题目形式

Question 27

The authors' use of the words "exact," "specific," and "complement" in lines 47-49 in the final paragraph functions mainly to

A) confirm that the nucleotide sequences are known for most molecules of DNA.

B) counter the claim that the sequences of bases along a chain can occur in any order.

C) support the claim that the phosphate-sugar backbone of the authors' model is completely regular.

D) emphasize how one chain of DNA may serve as a template to be copied during DNA replication.

★ 技巧真经

1. 扩展阅读上下文

回到原文单词所在句子，不能仅仅只读这句话，要扩展阅读上下文，才能理解句子的目的，从而理解作者使用该词汇的目的。

2. 把握强调目的

作者使用某些特定单词，或反复使用相似词义的单词，通常是为了强调某个观点和突出某种目的。去理解"作者想强调什么？"

3. 思考全文或段落中心

文中重要单词是为全文或该段中心服务的，是与中心一致的。把握中心大意，利于解题。

二、分析目的题（Analyzing Purpose）

分析目的题考查全文或某个段落或某些信息的写作目的。

题干标志词：the main purpose of … is to，…serves mainly to，function。

出题频率：高。

★ 题目形式

The main purpose of the first paragraph is to

A) describe a culture.

B) criticize a tradition.

C) question a suggestion.

D) analyze a reaction.

★ 技巧真经

1. 扩展阅读上下文

如果考段内某处信息的目的，要扩展阅读整个段落，理解段落中心；

如果考某个自然段的目的，要扩展阅读相邻的自然段，思考段落之间的逻辑关系；

如果考全文的写作目的，参考上一章全文中心题的技巧真经。

2. 抽象思维能力

分析目的题要求考生从文章具体文字描述的背后，抽象出写作目的。

要认真考查四个选项中抽象动词的词义区别，熟知下列单词：

criticize（批判）	question（质疑）	counter（反驳）	support（支持）
advocate（拥护）	acknowledge（承认）	confirm（确认）	present（提出）
provide（提供）	introduce（介绍）	describe（描述）	note（指出）
establish（建立）	analyze（分析）	validate（验证）	prove（证明）
explain（解释）	illustrate（阐明）	compare（对比）	emphasize（强调）

3. 区分内容和目的

干扰选项中有可能是某段内容的总结，但不是该段的写作目的。

BTW，做分析目的题，就是问自己："为什么作者要写这篇文章？" "为什么作者要写这个自然段？" "为什么作者要写这几句话？"

三、分析论点题（Analyzing Arguments）

分析论点题考查考生对全文作者中心论点或段落中分论点的把握。理解作者用什么样的写作手法去论证自己的观点或者驳斥反方观点。

题干标志词：claim（论点，宣称），counterclaim（反论点，反诉）。

出题频率：中。

⭐ 题目形式

The central claim of Passage 2 is that space mining has positive potential but

A) it will end up encouraging humanity's reckless treatment of the environment.

B) its effects should be thoughtfully considered before it becomes a reality.

C) such potential may not include replenishing key resources that are disappearing on Earth.

D) experts disagree about the commercial viability of the discoveries it could yield.

⭐ 技巧真经

1. 参考上一章全文中心题技巧真经

2. 关注文中证据、对比、结论

这些信息是用来支持和强调作者论点的，要重点考查以下 keywords 所在句子：

表示证据	**for example, because, statistics, surveys, case studies**
表达对比	**however, but, despite, on the contrary**
表达结论	**therefore, as a result, thus**

BTW，分析论点题和中心题非常相似，细微差别只是分析论点题更关注作者的主观思想。

四、分析态度题（Analyzing Point of View）

分析态度题考查对文中人物的立场、态度甚至偏见的把握。作者通过哪些写作手段、哪些词汇描写来透露出该人物的立场态度？

题干标志词：stance（立场），point of view，perspective（态度，角度）。

出题频率：低。

★ 题目形式

> The stance of Jordan takes in the passage is best described as that of
>
> A) an idealist setting forth principles.
>
> B) an advocate seeking a compromise position.
>
> C) an observer striving for neutrality.
>
> D) a scholar researching a historical controversy.

★ 技巧真经

1. 重点考查人物说话的细节

不仅要留意该人物说话的内容，还要留意说话的方式、语气强度。

相关句子中的形容词和副词是重要细节线索，因为形容词和副词常用来表达感情、程度、态度。

2. 参考上一章全文中心题技巧真经

除了重视细节之外，把握全文中心也会帮助解题。

BTW，分析人物态度题多出现在文学节选和演讲类文章中。

五、分析结构题（Analyzing Text Structure）

分析结构题考查对文章行文结构的把握。

有的文章结构单一，比如因果分析结构（cause-and-effect）、顺序结构（sequence），

或者提出问题给出解决方案的结构（problem-solution）；

也有的文章行文结构复杂或包含变化（shift），答案形式可能是：the passage begins by doing A and then doing B。

题干标志词：developmental pattern of the passage，over the course of the passage。

出题频率：低。

★ 题目形式

Over the course of the passage, the main focus of the narrative shifts from the

A) reservations a character has about a person he has just met to a growing appreciation that character has of the person's worth.

B) ambivalence a character feels about his sensitive nature to the character's recognition of the advantages of having profound emotions.

C) intensity of feeling a character has for another person to the character's concern that that intensity is not reciprocated.

D) value a character attaches to the wonders of the natural world to a rejection of that sort of beauty in favor of human artistry.

★ 技巧真经

1. 参考上一章全文中心题技巧真经

2. 注意自然段首句中的逻辑关系词

文章行文结构的变化，通常由某一自然段首句中的逻辑连词来表达，比如 but，after 等。

第四章

综合题（Syntheses）技巧真经

在真实的生活中，我们经常综合使用听说读写各项语言技能。所以在托福考试中，我们会碰到综合写作题，要求你先读、再听，最后结合你读到的和你听到的信息写一篇短文。

同样地，在真实生活中，我们也很少只通过一处信息来源就得出结论、做出决定。我们经常会综合各个渠道的信息，相互对比印证，最后得出更全面的、更客观的结论。

SAT 阅读的综合题就是培养对多来源信息的理解和处理能力。题目设计要么是考查对两篇短文的信息综合，要么是考查对文章文字信息和图表数据信息的综合。

所以，在 SAT 阅读中，综合题分为以下两类。

一、分析多文本题（Analyzing Multiple Texts）

二、分析数据信息题（Analyzing Quantitative Information）

一、分析多文本题（Analyzing Multiple Texts）

分析多文本题只针对双短文出题，考查理解两篇短文主旨之间的关系，或两篇短文中一处细节信息之间的对比关系。

题干标志词：passage 1, passage 2。

出题频率：中。

A. 双短文主旨关系题

⭐ 题目形式

> Which statement best describes the relationship between the passages?
>
> A) Passage 2 refutes the central claim advanced in Passage 1.
>
> B) Passage 2 illustrates the phenomenon described in more general terms in Passage 1.
>
> C) Passage 2 argues against the practicality of the proposals put forth in Passage 1.
>
> D) Passage 2 expresses reservations about developments discussed in Passage 1.

B. 双短文细节关系题

★ 题目形式

Which point about the resources that will be highly valued in space is implicit in Passage 1 and explicit in Passage 2?

A) They may be different resources from those that are valuable on Earth.

B) They will be valuable only if they can be harvested cheaply.

C) They are likely to be primarily precious metals and rare earth elements.

D) They may increase in value as those same resources become rare on Earth.

★ 技巧真经

1. 当成一篇长文章

首先从心理上克服对双短文这种陌生形式的排斥和恐惧。其实它就是把一篇长文章拆分成两部分而已。而且这篇长文章结构很清晰：前面几个自然段有一个分中心，后面几个自然段讲解另一个分中心论点，因此可以拆分成双短文。

2. 分别把握中心再对比

综合题都出现在最后，考生要利用前面的解题去深入理解两篇短文各自的内容重点、角度，把握各自的中心后，才可能对比理解出两者关系。关于短文中心思想的理解请参考第二章中心题技巧真经。

常见的双短文之间的对比关系有：**优势 Vs. 劣势；收益 Vs. 风险；理论 Vs. 实践；现象 Vs. 原因；问题 Vs. 办法**等。

3. 细节关系题画出原文出处

先分别在两篇短文中画出相应的细节信息出处，然后要通过上下文理解出细节信息所支持的观点（细节描写是为观点提供证据），最后再去对比。

二、分析数据信息题
（Analyzing Quantitative Information）

分析数据信息题针对数据图表出题，考查考生找出图表中具体信息、根据图表数据得出结论或综合图表数据和文章文字信息得出结论的能力。

题干标志词：graph, table, chart。

出题频率：中。

⭐ 题目形式

Do the data in the table support the authors' proposed pairing of bases in DNA?

A) Yes, because for each given organism, the percentage of adenine is closest to the percentage of thymine, and the percentage of guanine is closest to the percentage of cytosine.

B) Yes, because for each given organism, the percentage of adenine is closest to the percentage of guanine, and the percentage of cytosine is closest to the percentage of thymine.

C) No, because for each given organism, the percentage of adenine is closest to the percentage of thymine, and the percentage of guanine is closest to the percentage of cytosine.

D) No, because for each given organism, the percentage of adenine is closest to the percentage of guanine, and the percentage of cytosine is closest to the percentage of thymine.

★ 技巧真经

1. 图表信息支持文章

作者在文章后附上数据图表，这也是一种论证手段，用以支持自己的观点，不可能反驳文章（因此上题不可能选择 C、D 选项）。我们可以把图表信息看作一个例证自然段，在文中找出它要支持的观点。

2. 按正确顺序读图

不要一眼被众多的数据吸引。先看图表的表头标题，再看坐标轴的含义、图例的含义，最后再看具体数据，找出数据之间的共性、特性、交点、极值、趋势等，然后得出结论。

第五章

文学类文章真题精讲

一、总论

很多第一次接触 SAT 的考生翻开真题，看到了英文小说的节选。读了读，没读懂；一做题，什么鬼！？

同时，中国也有越来越多的中小学生，从小就培养用英文阅读儿童文学的习惯，比如经典童话，他们已经适应甚至喜欢上了。

比如我的孩子就喜爱阅读英语原版的《哈利·波特》，对于小说中一些精彩的章节和情节，他会翻来覆去地阅读，而且乐在其中。

我让他读了一篇 SAT 文章，也给他讲了讲。他觉得不过瘾，因为是节选，要求我给他买整本小说。

所以，一开始接触觉得难是很正常的，不要放弃。备考 SAT，说不定是一个机会、一个起点，让你从此多了一个爱好，喜欢上英美文学了呢？

★ 文章特点

● 中心不明确，具有大量的细节描写，包含对话和心理活动。

● 充满生动的比喻等修辞手法。

● 会碰到一定数量的生僻词汇和不熟悉的语法现象。

★ 技巧真经

● 重视文章前的引言介绍（画出 keywords），搞懂人物关系、小说背景（setting）。

● 阅读时重点思考各个角色的人物画像（人设）。

● 特别注意细节描写，比如人物说话时的语气、状态和心理活动。

● 留意各种状语，形容词、副词、介词短语等，体会感情色彩。

● 把握全文感情基调，读完文章后思考：你有什么样一种情绪？

下面，大家一起来学习《新 SAT 官方指南》Test 1 reading passage 1。建议自己先做一遍，然后再学习后面的真经派解析，以获得提高。

二、真题精讲

剧透花絮：

青年爱上了富家女。他登门请求女孩妈妈同意。

妈妈觉得：天啊，这小伙子好天真。

女儿却安静地说：妈妈，我要嫁给他。

请欣赏并享受下面这篇阅读文章，去看看青年男女敢于挑战世俗、追求爱情的勇气，并被这种青春纯真的力量所感动。

"你不是在读英语，你要学会用英语去阅读，去享受，去被感动。"

这句话是我对孩子说的，也送给你。

★ Reading Test

65 MINUTES, 52 QUESTIONS

Turn to Section 1 of your answer sheet to answer the questions in this section.

DIRECTIONS

Each passage or pair of passages below is followed by a number of questions. After reading each passage or pair, choose the best answer to each question based on what is stated or implied in the passage or passages and in any accompanying graphics (such as a table or graph).

Questions 1–10 are based on the following passage.

This passage is from Lydia Minatoya, *The Strangeness of Beauty*. ©1999 by Lydia Minatoya. The setting is Japan in 1920. Chie and her daughter Naomi are members of the House of Fuji, a noble family.

Line Akira came directly, breaking all tradition. Was that it? Had he followed form—had he asked his mother to speak to his father to approach a go-between—would Chie have been more receptive?

5 He came on a winter's eve. He pounded on the door while a cold rain beat on the shuttered veranda, so at first Chie thought him only the wind. The maid knew better. Chie heard her soft scuttling footsteps, the creak of the door. Then the maid brought a
10 calling card to the drawing room, for Chie.

Chie was reluctant to go to her guest; perhaps she was feeling too cozy. She and Naomi were reading at a low table set atop a charcoal brazier. A thick quilt spread over the sides of the table so their legs were
15 tucked inside with the heat.

"Who is it at this hour, in this weather?" Chie questioned as she picked the name card off the maid's lacquer tray.

"Shinoda, Akira. Kobe Dental College," she read.

20 Naomi recognized the name. Chie heard a soft intake of air.

"I think you should go," said Naomi.

Akira was waiting in the entry. He was in his early twenties, slim and serious, wearing the black
25 military-style uniform of a student. As he bowed—his hands hanging straight down, a black cap in one, a yellow oil-paper umbrella in the other—Chie glanced beyond him. In the glistening surface of the courtyard's rain-drenched paving
30 stones, she saw his reflection like a dark double.

"Madame," said Akira, "forgive my disruption, but I come with a matter of urgency."

His voice was soft, refined. He straightened and stole a deferential peek at her face.

35 In the dim light his eyes shone with sincerity. Chie felt herself starting to like him.

"Come inside, get out of this nasty night. Surely your business can wait for a moment or two."

"I don't want to trouble you. Normally I would
40 approach you more properly but I've received word of a position. I've an opportunity to go to America, as dentist for Seattle's Japanese community."

"Congratulations," Chie said with amusement. "That is an opportunity, I'm sure. But how am I
45 involved?"

Even noting Naomi's breathless reaction to the name card, Chie had no idea. Akira's message, delivered like a formal speech, filled her with maternal amusement. You know how children speak

50 so earnestly, so hurriedly, so endearingly about things that have no importance in an adult's mind? That's how she viewed him, as a child.

It was how she viewed Naomi. Even though Naomi was eighteen and training endlessly in the arts
55 needed to make a good marriage, Chie had made no effort to find her a husband.

Akira blushed.

"Depending on your response, I may stay in Japan. I've come to ask for Naomi's hand."

60 Suddenly Chie felt the dampness of the night.

"Does Naomi know anything of your... ambitions?"

"We have an understanding. Please don't judge my candidacy by the unseemliness of this proposal. I
65 ask directly because the use of a go-between takes much time. Either method comes down to the same thing: a matter of parental approval. If you give your consent, I become Naomi's yoshi. * We'll live in the House of Fuji. Without your consent, I must go to
70 America, to secure a new home for my bride."

Eager to make his point, he'd been looking her full in the face. Abruptly, his voice turned gentle. "I see I've startled you. My humble apologies. I'll take no more of your evening. My address is on my card. If
75 you don't wish to contact me, I'll reapproach you in two weeks' time. Until then, good night."

He bowed and left. Taking her ease, with effortless grace, like a cat making off with a fish.

"Mother?" Chie heard Naomi's low voice and
80 turned from the door. "He has asked you?"

The sight of Naomi's clear eyes, her dark brows gave Chie strength. Maybe his hopes were preposterous.

"Where did you meet such a fellow? Imagine! He
85 thinks he can marry the Fuji heir and take her to America all in the snap of his fingers!"

Chie waited for Naomi's ripe laughter.

Naomi was silent. She stood a full half minute looking straight into Chie's eyes. Finally, she spoke.
90 "I met him at my literary meeting."

Naomi turned to go back into the house, then stopped.

"Mother."

"Yes?"

95 "I mean to have him."

* a man who marries a woman of higher status and takes her family's name

1

Which choice best describes what happens in the passage?

A) One character argues with another character who intrudes on her home.

B) One character receives a surprising request from another character.

C) One character reminisces about choices she has made over the years.

D) One character criticizes another character for pursuing an unexpected course of action.

2

Which choice best describes the developmental pattern of the passage?

A) A careful analysis of a traditional practice

B) A detailed depiction of a meaningful encounter

C) A definitive response to a series of questions

D) A cheerful recounting of an amusing anecdote

3

As used in line 1 and line 65, "directly" most nearly means

A) frankly.

B) confidently.

C) without mediation.

D) with precision.

4

Which reaction does Akira most fear from Chie?

A) She will consider his proposal inappropriate.

B) She will mistake his earnestness for immaturity.

C) She will consider his unscheduled visit an imposition.

D) She will underestimate the sincerity of his emotions.

5

Which choice provides the best evidence for the answer to the previous question?

A) Line 33 ("His voice... refined")

B) Lines 49–51 ("You... mind")

C) Lines 63–64 ("Please... proposal")

D) Lines 71–72 ("Eager... face")

6

In the passage, Akira addresses Chie with

A) affection but not genuine love.

B) objectivity but not complete impartiality.

C) amusement but not mocking disparagement.

D) respect but not utter deference.

7

The main purpose of the first paragraph is to

A) describe a culture.

B) criticize a tradition.

C) question a suggestion.

D) analyze a reaction.

8

As used in line 2, "form" most nearly means

A) appearance.

B) custom.

C) structure.

D) nature.

9

Why does Akira say his meeting with Chie is "a matter of urgency" (line 32)?

A) He fears that his own parents will disapprove of Naomi.

B) He worries that Naomi will reject him and marry someone else.

C) He has been offered an attractive job in another country.

D) He knows that Chie is unaware of his feelings for Naomi.

10

Which choice provides the best evidence for the answer to the previous question?

A) Line 39 ("I don't... you")

B) Lines 39–42 ("Normally... community")

C) Lines 58–59 ("Depending... Japan")

D) Lines 72–73 ("I see... you")

⭐ 真经派精讲

Question 1

Which choice best describes what happens in the passage?

A) One character argues with another character who intrudes on her home.

B) One character receives a surprising request from another character.

C) One character reminisces about choices she has made over the years.

D) One character criticizes another character for pursuing an unexpected course of action.

1. 答案

B) 一个人物角色接收到来自另一个角色的一个令人吃惊的要求。

2. 精讲

总结题。可以最后再做。

选项中的 one character 指的是母亲 Chie；another character 指的是青年 Akira。

考点设计就是对 B 选项中 surprising request 的理解。

既然是对全文的总结，考点信息的对应就不只是一处，全文多处都在表达 surprising request。

原文第 47 行："Chie had no idea"表明母亲（丈母娘）以前都不知道这位青年（准女婿）的存在，对青年的名字和接下来要提的要求一无所知。为后面的 surprising 做了铺垫。

原文第 59 行："I've come to ask for Naomi's hand"；

原文第 64 行："...of this proposal."

以上两处中 ask for 和 proposal 对应了选项中的 request 一词。

当听到青年提出了 request，母亲的第一反应来自原文第 60 行："Suddenly Chie felt the dampness of the night"。

注意 Suddenly 一词本身就表达出"意料之外、吃惊"的感觉了。

而且后面的表达中，即使考生不认识 dampness（潮湿）一词，通过句意："突然，Chie 感受到了夜的 ××。"也可猜到，dampness 的意思不是"黑"，就是"冷，湿冷"。还记得文章前面的环境描写吗？ winter's eve, cold rain。

冬夜、冷雨。

在家里温暖的火盆边读书，被迫出门接待一位不速之客。

听完了他的要求，突然，感到了夜的湿冷。

你看，作家对这场对话的环境设定是精心的、有预谋的。

另外，原文第 72 行："I see I've startled you." 我明白我吓着您了。注意 startled（惊吓）一词。

原文第 77 行："Taking her ease" 带走了她的平静。注意 ease 和 surprising 的词义对立。

以上这些，都在对应选项中 surprising request 的表达，你都找到了吗？

干扰选项排除：A 选项中的 argue（争论）、intrude（闯入）和 D 选项中的 criticize（批评），这三个词都比较激烈和负面，不准确。原文中青年礼貌地表达完自己的要求，优雅地离开，留下了女孩的母亲独自吃惊。C 选项说一个角色 reminisce（回忆）多年来她做过的选择。选项内容与文章相关性更差，可最先轻松排除。

BTW，其实，《新 SAT 官方指南》——*The official SAT Study Guide* 一书中附有英文版解析，但我为什么还要费神写真经派的精讲解析呢？下面附本题官方解析，看完，对比，你可能就理解了：因为流派不同，教学法就不同。

Question 1

Choice B is the best answer. In the passage, a young man (Akira) asks a mother (Chie) for permission to marry her daughter (Naomi). The request was certainly surprising to the mother, as can be seen from line 47, which states that prior to Akira's question Chie "had no idea" the request was coming.

Choice A is incorrect because the passage depicts two characters engaged in a civil conversation, with Chie being impressed with Akira's "sincerity" and finding herself "starting to like him." Choice C is incorrect because the passage is focused on the idea of Akira's and Naomi's present lives and possible futures. Choice D is incorrect because the interactions between Chie and Akira are polite, not critical; for example, Chie views Akira with "amusement," not animosity.

Question 2

Which choice best describes the developmental pattern of the passage?

A) A careful analysis of a traditional practice

B) A detailed depiction of a meaningful encounter

C) A definitive response to a series of questions

D) A cheerful recounting of an amusing anecdote

1. 答案

B) 对一次重要见面的详细描写。

2. 精讲

分析结构题。

上一题是总结文章的内容，这一题是总结文章的结构，这两道题具有相关性。做对第 1 题对快速做对本题有很大帮助。

第 1 题的正确选项揭示了文章描述一个人物角色向另一位人物提出一个吃惊的要求。那么这个要求是在什么场合提出的呢？就是在一个 meaningful（重要的，有意义的）encounter（会面，碰面）中。而且作家对这次 encounter 的时间、地点、天气，双方的对话、心理活动等进行了 detailed（细节的）depiction（描述）。因此，本题的正确选项 B 应该快速地被选出。

干扰选项排除：A 选项中的 traditional practice 原文有提到，但并没有 careful analysis（仔细分析）。C 选项中 definitive（决定性的）response（回应）不对。原文中母亲没有对青年提出的要求或者问题给出明确回应。D 选项 a cheerful（令人愉快的）recounting（讲述）of an amusing（有趣的）anecdote（趣闻、逸事）。这个选项是来"打酱油"的，排除。

> **Question 3**
>
> As used in line 1 and line 65, "directly" most nearly means
>
> A) frankly.
>
> B) confidently.
>
> C) without mediation.
>
> D) with precision.

1. 答案

C) 没有中间人。

2. 精讲

词义题。

容易错选 A 选项。因为 directly（直接地）和 frankly（坦白地、直率地）这两个词考生很熟悉，我们口语经常使用 frankly speaking 这个表达，而且这两个单词词义确实相近，一些场合下可以替换。

但请一定牢记，SAT 阅读中的词义题是考查该词在上下文中的词义。原文第 65 行：I ask directly because the use of a go-between takes much time. 注意到上下文因果关系，显然该题目要考查对 go-between 一词的理解。其实从字面意思猜测，go-between 是"两者之间，中间"的含义，已经可以怀疑是否对应 C 选项的 mediation 一词了。

如果你对 go-between 一词有印象，其实在文章首段就出现过一次，首段也同时出现了 directly 一词。再加上阅读完文章之后，我们知道了青年打破传统，直接上门向女孩的母亲提亲，没有让自己的父母去 approach（接洽、找）一个 go-between，我们就可以猜到该词的含义：go-between（媒人、红娘、中间人）。

所以，原文中 directly 一词强调的不是坦诚、坦白，而是强调了 without mediation（没有中间人）。少年认为找中间人、媒人浪费时间。

就像瓜子二手车广告"没有中间商赚差价"，强调的是没有 go-between，不是强调自己的价格是明码标价，很 frank（坦白、直率）。

干扰选项是 B) confidently（自信地，有把握地）和 D) with precision（精确地）。这两个选项的设计很没有诚意，"打酱油"都不认真。

Question 4

Which reaction does Akira most fear from Chie?

A) She will consider his proposal inappropriate.

B) She will mistake his earnestness for immaturity.

C) She will consider his unscheduled visit an imposition.

D) She will underestimate the sincerity of his emotions.

1. 答案

A) 她会认为他的提亲是不恰当的。

Question 5

Which choice provides the best evidence for the answer to the previous question?

A) Line 33 ("His voice... refined")

B) Lines 49–51 ("You... mind")

C) Lines 63–64 ("Please... proposal")

D) Lines 71–72 ("Eager... face")

---

1. 答案

答案：C)

2. 精讲

这是一组细读题和引证题的组合。

就像在本书第二章我们讲到的这种组合题的技巧：当对前一题我们一头雾水、不知道从原文哪里去寻找线索时，可以先读后面一道引证题，四个选项就是四条线索，其中一条必然是正确的线索。

第 4 题较难，问青年 most fear（最担心）母亲有什么反应。我们如果无法准确确定原文出处，就先做第 5 题，按第 5 题四个选项的指引，分别仔细阅读原文中的那四句话。

当按照第 5 题 C 选项的指引，读到"Please don't..."的时候，显然这个 please don't 表达的语气对应第 4 题题干中的 fear 一词。

所以，先将第 5 题选出 C 选项，再认真读原文中"Please don't..."这句话的上下文，去理解少年到底担心的是什么。

原文："Please don't judge my candidacy by the unseemliness of this proposal. I ask directly because the use of a go-between takes much time."

注意句中 candidacy（候选人资格）和 umseemliness（不适宜的，唐突的）这两个词。原文大意为：请不要因为我这么唐突的提亲方式而质疑我的求婚资格。我这么直接是因为通过媒人太费时间。

所以，青年担心的是自己这种打破传统、不得体的提亲方式让女方的母亲产生质疑。他还给出了自己的解释，省掉媒人是要想加快时间，并非故意唐突。第 4 题 A 选项中关键词 proposal 和 inappropriate（不恰当）一一对应。

干扰选项 B 中关键词 earnestness（真诚）、immaturity（不成熟），C 选项中 unscheduled visit（未事先计划的拜访），D 选项中 sincerity（真诚）、emotions（感情）都不正确。

Question 6

In the passage, Akira addresses Chie with

A) affection but not genuine love.

B) objectivity but not complete impartiality.

C) amusement but not mocking disparagement.

D) respect but not utter deference.

---

1. 答案

D) 尊重但不是彻底遵从。

2. 精讲

分析态度题。

首先注意题干中 address 一词作动词，此处词义是"应对"。

题目问：文章中，青年在应对女方母亲时的态度是什么。

这是一道应对原文多处信息的总结题。如果原文阅读比较好，选项中单词理解没有障碍，可以直接选出正确选项。而且，其他三个干扰选项迷惑性不大。

A 选项，青年和女方母亲第一次见面谈不上 affection（喜爱）和 love。

B 选项，提亲谈不上 objectivity（客观）或是否 impartiality（不偏不倚）。如果你将来碰到非常理智、客观、不带强烈主观情绪的求婚，千万不要答应！

C 选项，amusement（娱乐）？他敢吗？我就问谁敢这样对待未来的丈母娘？有没有"贵粉儿"选这个选项，出来走两步我看看？哈哈。

只有 D 选项 respect（尊重）合理。原文中有多处细节体现：he bowed, Madame, forgive my disruption, deferential（恭敬的）peek（偷看），my humble apologies 等。

但青年对女方母亲是不是 utter（完全地、彻底地）deference（遵从、听从）呢？

不是的。他打破传统而来，而且在谈话中，他表达如果女方母亲同意，他留在日本；如果不同意，他也要和女孩去美国生活。最后他走的时候，还说：如果你不想联系我，我两周后再来。

Question 7

The main purpose of the first paragraph is to

A) describe a culture.

B) criticize a tradition.

C) question a suggestion.

D) analyze a reaction.

1. 答案

D) 分析一个反应。

2. 精讲

这是修辞题中的分析目的题，有难度。

既然是分析写作的目的，就不会局限在表面上读到的文字内容，需要深入思考。

第一段说：青年打破了传统。如果他遵循传统方式 —— 通过父母找一个媒人去提亲 —— 女方母亲是不是会更 receptive（容易接受）一些呢？

我们注意到第一段字面上的确介绍了日本提亲的文化风俗，但这是作者写这个自然段的目的吗？

第 1 段最后一句笔墨最重，用的是一个虚拟语气。通过这个虚拟语气的句子，作者暗示了青年这次打破传统的提亲效果并不理想。女方母亲的 reaction（反应）并不是 more receptive。

所以，对日本提亲风俗的描写，是为了分析和说明原因：为什么女方母亲的反应不理想。显然对应了 D 选项。

三个干扰选项都有迷惑性。culture，tradition，suggestion 这三个词感觉都和内容沾边，尤其是 A 选项。A 选项中 culture 一词太大，但即使把 A 选项改成 describe a tradition，也不能选，因为第 1 段确实描写了一种传统，但这不是作者的写作目的。

Question 8

As used in line 2, "form" most nearly means

A) appearance.

B) custom.

C) structure.

D) nature.

1. 答案

B) custom 习俗。

2. 精讲

简单的词义题。

注意到原文 form 后面是破折号，两个破折号之间的内容是对 form 的解释说明。通过破折号之间的信息可以大致判断 form 是一种方式、方法、形式。再通过上下文，break tradition 和 follow form 表达对立，可以判断文中 form 和 tradition 是同义词。

Question 9

Why does Akira say his meeting with Chie is "a matter of urgency" (line 32)?

A) He fears that his own parents will disapprove of Naomi.

B) He worries that Naomi will reject him and marry someone else.

C) He has been offered an attractive job in another country.

D) He knows that Chie is unaware of his feelings for Naomi.

1. 答案

C) 他得到一个在国外有吸引力的工作机会。

Question 10

Which choice provides the best evidence for the answer to the previous question?

A) Line 39 ("I don't... you")

B) Lines 39–42 ("Normally... community")

C) Lines 58–59 ("Depending... Japan")

D) Lines 72–73 ("I see... you")

1. 答案

B)

2. 精讲

这又是一个细读题和引证题组合，但这个组合比第 4 题和第 5 题的组合简单多了。因为第 9 题的题干中有明确的定位指引：line 32。

回到原文第 32 行，找到 urgency（紧急），然后阅读上下文去找青年认为这件事很紧急的原因。往下读到第 39 行，少年解释道："I don't want to trouble you. Normally I would approach you more properly but I've received word of a position. I've an opportunity to go to America, as dentist for Seattle's Japanese community."

注意到转折结构 but 后面就是紧急的原因：他获得了一个海外的工作职位，他需要做出选择。

注意 C 选项中 offer 对应原文中 receive；job 对应 position；another country 对应 America；attractive 对应 opportunity。有没有一种明察秋毫的感觉？哈哈。

请回忆并复习一下本书第二章中真经派技巧：直接细读题，难度低，找出正确选项和原文间的多组同义替换。

由于第 9 题定位简单，题型简单，按真经派的同义替换原则我们可以 100% 确认 C)选项正确，根本不需要在其他三个干扰选项上费时纠结。

第 9 题完成后，我们再花费宝贵的 1 秒钟时间，给第 10 题选出 B 选项，哈哈。

★ 参考译文

本文节选自 1999 年 Lydia Minatoya 的《美之惊异》。小说的背景发生在 1920 年的日本。Chie 和她的女儿 Naomi 是日本非常显赫的富士家族成员。

Akira 直接上门拜访，这打破了一切传统。这算怎么回事儿呢？如果 Akira 遵循传统，通过他的母亲让他的父亲找一个媒人，那么 Chie 会不会更容易接受一些呢？

那是一个冬夜。当寒冷的冬雨敲打着合着百叶窗的走廊时，他敲响了门，以至于 Chie 起初认为门外只是风声。女佣的反应更敏捷些，Chie 听到女佣轻柔急促的脚步声和吱呀的开门声，接着一张名片就被送到了客厅，是给 Chie 的。

Chie 不愿意去见她的客人，或许是因为她不想破坏现在舒适的状态。她和 Naomi 正在矮桌旁读书，桌子下面放了一个温暖的火盆。一条厚被子展开横铺，盖住桌边，她们正好可以把腿塞进去取暖。

"这个点了，这样的坏天气，会是谁呢？"当她从女佣的漆制托盘中拿起名片的时候，Chie 问道。

"Shinoda, Akira。神户牙科学院，"她读道。

Naomi 知道这个名字。Chie 听到她轻轻地吸了一口气。

"我认为你该去见见，"Naomi 说。

Akira 站在门口等着。他二十岁出头，身材高挑，面色严肃，穿着一身黑色的军装样式的学校校服。当他鞠躬的时候，他的两手垂直向下，一只手里拿着一顶黑色的帽子，另一只手里拿着一把黄色的油纸伞。Chie 瞟了他身后一眼。庭院里雨水浸湿的石板路散发着闪闪的光，映射出他深色的倒影。

"夫人，"Akira 说，"请原谅我的打扰，但是，我真的有很紧急的事。"

他的声音既柔和又很优雅。他挺直站着，偷偷地看了一下 Chie 的脸，眼神中充满尊重。

在昏暗的灯光下，他的眼睛闪烁着真诚。Chie 觉得她开始喜欢这个年轻人了。

"进来吧，别再站在这糟糕的雨夜里了。我相信你要跟我说的事也不急于这一时半会儿。"

"我不想打搅您的。我本该以更体面的方式拜访您，但是我已得知我获得了一个职位。我可以去美国，在西雅图的日本城做一名牙科医生。"

"恭喜，"Chie 开心地说，"我相信那确实是一个机会。但是，这和我有什么关联吗？"

即使留意到女儿见到名片时窒息般的反应，Chie 依然是一无所知。Akira 带来的信息，就像一次正式的演讲，让她充满了母亲般的喜悦。你知道当一个孩子如此真诚、如此急切、如此惹人怜爱地给一个成年人讲述一些在成年人心目中并不重要的东西时的情形吗？在她眼中，他就是如此，像一个孩子。

她也是这样看待 Naomi 的。即使她已经 18 岁了，并且正在没完没了地训练那些嫁个好人家需要的技艺，Chie 也从没试图给她找一个丈夫。

Akira 脸红了。

"这取决于您的态度，我可以待在日本。我来是想求您把 Naomi 嫁给我。"

Chie 突然感受到了夜的凉意。

"Naomi 知道你的想法吗？"

"我们之间是有默契的。请您不要因为我这么唐突的求婚方式而质疑我的诚心。我这么直接是因为通过媒人太费时间。其实，两种方法的目的都是一样的：希望得到父母的许可。如果您同意，我会入赘。我们将生活在富士家。如果您不同意，我必须去美国，在那里安置好一个新家去迎接我的新娘。"

因为太过急切于想要表达清楚自己的观点，他直直地盯着她的脸。突然，他的声音变得柔和起来。"我明白我吓着您了。我请求您的原谅。我也不便再占用您的时间了。名片上有我的地址。如果您不想主动联系我，我两周后再来拜访您。到时候见，晚安。"

他鞠了一躬，然后离开。像猫偷走鱼那样，他轻而易举地就让 Chie 不安起来。

"妈妈，"听见 Naomi 低声地询问，Chie 转身。"他已经问过您了吗？"

看到 Naomi 清澈的眼睛和浓黑的眉毛，她又恢复了冷静。或许，他的想法是可笑的。

"你是在哪遇到这样一个小伙子的？天哪！他居然认为他打一个响指就可以迎娶富士家族的继承人并把她带到美国去！"

Chie 期待着 Naomi 世故的笑声。

Naomi 沉默不语。她站在那里足有半分钟，直直地看着 Chie 的眼睛。最后，她开口道："我是在文学会上遇见他的。"

她转身走回房间，接着，停下脚步。

"妈妈。"

"什么事？"

"我要嫁给他。"

第六章

历史社会类文章真题精讲

一、总论

SAT 阅读的历史社会类文章一共两篇，或者一篇加上双短文。从主题上看也分为两种：社会科学类文章，如：经济、心理学、社会学；历史文献类文章，如：美国建国文献或国际知名演讲节选。

社会科学类文章结构清晰，内容和我们日常生活相关，应该是 SAT 阅读中难度最低的文章。相关特点和技巧真经，请参考第七章科学类文章真题精讲的总论。

相反，美国建国文献类文章，诸如权利法案、独立宣言、联邦党人文集等，对中国考生来说难度较大，主要是因为**背景不熟和文化差异**。试想一下，如果不知道美国国会的构成和职能，如果不清楚 impeachment（弹劾）这一词背后牵涉的美国政党制的游戏规则，就很难真正理解上下文。

同样，阅读知名演讲稿也是一个要攻克的难关。这种文章中作者（演讲者）为了增强语言的说服力，会用到**抽象的比喻、巧妙的设问、气势磅礴的排比**等修辞手法，很容易让考生迷失阅读的重心和逻辑。

★ 文章特点

● 美国建国文献类文章，背景不熟和文化差异导致理解障碍。

● 演讲类文章口语化表达和修辞手法较多。

● 多讨论诸如公平、权利等抽象理念，词汇抽象，句子结构复杂。

★ 技巧真经

● 重视文章前的引言介绍（画出 keywords），理解背景。

● 越是内容不熟、满篇修辞的文章，越要找出每段中心句。

- 注意文章中的逻辑关联词，找出行文推进线索。

下面，大家一起来学习《新 SAT 官方指南》Test 1 reading passage 3。建议自己先做一遍，再学习后面的真经派解析，以获得提高。

二、真题精讲 1

剧透花絮：

"书中自有黄金屋"，这句话不是夸张和比喻。

每个人的一生中，总会花很多钱在买礼物上。读完下面这篇文章，你会发现：为什么人们收到越昂贵的礼物反而可能越不高兴？

"礼轻情意重"这句中国古话蕴藏的智慧，西方用经济学、人类学、社会心理学的理论和统计数据图表来进行了验证。

下面这篇社会科学类文章其实是一篇财富秘笈：省省钱，反而到达更好的效果。

"读书让你感觉每天在成长；不读书你每天只是在老去。"

这句话是我对学为贵集团全体同事说的，也送给你。

Questions 11–21 are based on the following passage and supplementary material.

This passage is adapted from Francis J. Flynn and Gabrielle S. Adams, *Money Can't Buy Love: Asymmetric Beliefs about Gift Price and Feelings of Appreciation.* ©2008 by Elsevier Inc.

Line　　Every day, millions of shoppers hit the stores
　　　　in full force—both online and on foot—searching
　　　　frantically for the perfect gift. Last year, Americans
　　　　spent over $30 billion at retail stores in the
　　5　　month of December alone. Aside from purchasing
　　　　holiday gifts, most people regularly buy presents
　　　　for other occasions throughout the year, including
　　　　weddings, birthdays, anniversaries, graduations,
　　　　and baby showers. This frequent experience of gift-
　10　　giving can engender ambivalent feelings in gift-
　　　　givers. Many relish the opportunity to buy presents
　　　　because gift-giving offers a powerful means to
　　　　build stronger bonds with one's closest peers. At
　　　　the same time, many dread the thought of buying
　15　　gifts; they worry that their purchases will disappoint
　　　　rather than delight the intended recipients.

　　　　　Anthropologists describe gift-giving as a positive
　　　　social process, serving various political, religious,
　　　　and psychological functions. Economists, however,
　20　　offer a less favorable view. According to Waldfogel
　　　　(1993), gift-giving represents an objective waste of
　　　　resources. People buy gifts that recipients would not
　　　　choose to buy on their own, or at least not spend as
　　　　much money to purchase (a phenomenon referred
　25　　to as "the deadweight loss of Christmas"). To wit,
　　　　givers are likely to spend $100 to purchase a gift that
　　　　receivers would spend only $80 to buy themselves.

This "deadweight loss" suggests that gift-givers are not very good at predicting what gifts others will
30　appreciate. That in itself is not surprising to social psychologists. Research has found that people often struggle to take account of others' perspectives—their insights are subject to egocentrism, social projection, and multiple attribution errors.

35　　What is surprising is that gift-givers have considerable experience acting as both gift-givers and gift-recipients, but nevertheless tend to overspend each time they set out to purchase a meaningful gift. In the present research, we
40　propose a unique psychological explanation for this overspending problem—i.e., that gift-givers equate how much they spend with how much recipients will appreciate the gift (the more expensive the gift, the stronger a gift-recipient's feelings of
45　appreciation). Although a link between gift price and feelings of appreciation might seem intuitive to gift-givers, such an assumption may be unfounded. Indeed, we propose that gift-recipients will be less inclined to base their feelings of appreciation on
50　the magnitude of a gift than givers assume.

　　Why do gift-givers assume that gift price is closely linked to gift-recipients' feelings of appreciation? Perhaps givers believe that bigger (i.e., more expensive) gifts convey stronger signals
55　of thoughtfulness and consideration. According to Camerer (1988) and others, gift-giving represents a symbolic ritual, whereby gift-givers attempt to signal their positive attitudes toward the intended recipient and their willingness to invest resources in a future
60　relationship. In this sense, gift-givers may be motivated

to spend more money on a gift in order to send a "stronger signal" to their intended recipient. As for gift-recipients, they may not construe smaller and larger gifts as representing smaller and larger

65 signals of thoughtfulness and consideration.

The notion of gift-givers and gift-recipients being unable to account for the other party's perspective seems puzzling because people slip in and out of these roles every day, and, in some cases,

70 multiple times in the course of the same day. Yet, despite the extensive experience that people have as both givers and receivers, they often struggle to transfer information gained from one role (e.g., as a giver) and apply it in another, complementary role

75 (e.g., as a receiver). In theoretical terms, people fail to utilize information about their own preferences and experiences in order to produce more efficient outcomes in their exchange relations. In practical terms, people spend hundreds of dollars each year

80 on gifts, but somehow never learn to calibrate their gift expenditures according to personal insight.

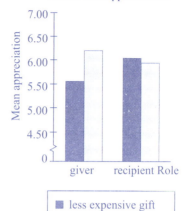

Givers' Perceived and Recipients' Actual Gift Appreciations

less expensive gift
more expensive gift

11

The authors most likely use the
examples in lines 1–9 of the passage
("Every…showers") to highlight the
A) regularity with which people shop
   for gifts.
B) recent increase in the amount of money
   spent on gifts.
C) anxiety gift shopping causes for
   consumers.
D) number of special occasions involving
   gift-giving.

12

In line 10, the word "ambivalent" most
nearly means
A) unrealistic.
B) conflicted.
C) apprehensive.
D) supportive.

13

The authors indicate that people value
gift-giving because they feel it
A) functions as a form of self-expression.
B) is an inexpensive way to show
   appreciation.
C) requires the gift-recipient to
   reciprocate.
D) can serve to strengthen a relationship.

14

Which choice provides the best evidence
   for the answer to the previous
   question?
A) Lines 11–13 ("Many…peers")
B) Lines 22–23 ("People…own")
C) Lines 31–32 ("Research…perspectives")
D) Lines 45–47 ("Although…unfounded")

15

The "social psychologists" mentioned
in paragraph 2 (lines 17–34) would
likely describe the "deadweight loss"
phenomenon as
A) predictable.
B) questionable.
C) disturbing.
D) unprecedented.

16

The passage indicates that the assumption made by gift-givers in lines 41–44 may be

A) insincere.

B) unreasonable.

C) incorrect.

D) substantiated.

17

Which choice provides the best evidence for the answer to the previous question?

A) Lines 53–55 ("Perhaps… consideration")

B) Lines 55–60 ("According…relationship")

C) Lines 62–65 ("As…consideration")

D) Lines 75–78 ("In…relations")

18

As it is used in line 54, "convey" most nearly means

A) transport.

B) counteract.

C) exchange.

D) communicate.

19

The authors refer to work by Camerer and others (line 56) in order to

A) offer an explanation.

B) introduce an argument.

C) question a motive.

D) support a conclusion.

20

The graph following the passage offers evidence that gift-givers base their predictions of how much a gift will be appreciated on

A) the appreciation level of the gift-recipients.

B) the monetary value of the gift.

C) their own desires for the gifts they purchase.

D) their relationship with the gift-recipients.

21

The authors would likely attribute the differences in gift-giver and recipient mean appreciation as represented in the graph to

A) an inability to shift perspective.

B) An increasingly materialistic culture.

C) A growing opposition to gift-giving.

D) A misunderstanding of intentions.

★ 真经派精讲

Question 11

The authors most likely use the examples in lines 1–9 of the passage ("Every... showers") to highlight the

A) regularity with which people shop for gifts.

B) recent increase in the amount of money spent on gifts.

C) anxiety gift shopping causes for consumers.

D)　number of special occasions involving gift-giving.

1. 答案

A) 人们买礼物的经常性。

2. 精讲

分析目的题。

原文第 1–9 行讲到：每天很多人（millions）买礼物。人们花很多钱（billions）买礼物。除了节日，人们在各种场合经常买礼物。

内容提到：人多、花钱多、频率高。总结就是美国人爱买礼物，经常买礼物。所以对应 A 选项中的 regularity 一词。该题不难，原文第 6 行已经出现了 regularly 一词。

干扰选项 B 中的 recent increase 原文没有提及和对比；C 选项中的 anxiety（焦虑）原文第 1–9 行没有提及；D 选项的细节内容原文有，但不是作者想 highlight（强调）的观点。

Question 12

In line 10, the word "ambivalent" most nearly means

A) unrealistic.

B) conflicted.

C) apprehensive.

D) supportive.

1. 答案

B) 矛盾的。

2. 精讲

词义题，考查上下文逻辑。

原文第 10 行提到 ambivalent feelings，这是什么 feelings 呢？读下一句，注意这两句话之间没有逻辑关联词，那么通常下一句的内容和上一句自然承接，进一步解释说明。

下一句中提到 many relish; 再下一句说到：At the same time, many dread。显然，ambivalent feelings 包含了 relish 和 dread 两层内容。但我们又不认识 relish 和 dread 这两个单词，那又该怎么办呢？

仔细阅读 Many relish the opportunity 这句话，发现因果关系 because，我们至少读得懂原因后面是好事，那么结果也是好事。所以 relish 一词是指好事。

再仔细阅读下一句，At the same time，发现 dread 一词虽然不熟，但句中出现了 worry 一词，显然 dread 一词是指坏事。

所以，ambivalent feeling 包含了 relish（享受、喜欢）好事，at the same time，又

包含了 dread（害怕、担心）坏事。所以答案选出 B 选项 conflicted（矛盾的，冲突的）。

其实单词 ambivalent（喜忧参半的）的前缀很常见，ambi- 指的是 both，around 的含义。常见的有：ambiguous（模棱两可的）；ambitious（有抱负的，野心勃勃的），该词前缀指 around（到处，四处），字根 it 指 go（走）。所以，好男儿志在四方，全世界走走，出国留学，就是有 ambition。

其他三个干扰选项词义为：A) unrealistic（不切实际的）；C) apprehensive（担忧的）；D) supportive（支持的，给予帮助的）。

> **Question 13**
>
> The authors indicate that people value gift-giving because they feel it
>
> A) functions as a form of self-expression.
>
> B) is an inexpensive way to show appreciation.
>
> C) requires the gift-recipient to reciprocate.
>
> D) can serve to strengthen a relationship.

1. 答案

D) 能用来加强关系。

> **Question 14**
>
> Which choice provides the best evidence for the answer to the previous question?
>
> A) Lines 11–13 ("Many...peers")
>
> B) Lines 22–23 ("People...own")
>
> C) Lines 31–32 ("Research...perspectives")
>
> D) Lines 45–47 ("Although...unfounded")

1. 答案

A)

2. 精讲

细读题和引证题组合。

命题"友好"而简单。因为刚做完第 12 题，对原文第 10 行的句子还有印象。注意用第 13 题题干中 because 一词，因果关系关键词定位，可以再次回到原文第 11 行，看到 because 原词出现。然后细读句子发现：

relish the opportunity 对应题干中的 value（重视）这个动词；

offers 对应 D 选项中的 serve（提供）；

powerful, stronger 对应 D 选项中的 strengthen（加强）；

build bonds（纽带，关系）对应 D 选项中的 relationship。

回忆并复习直接细读题的真经技巧：多组同义替换。

又是明察秋毫的感觉。

当完成第 13 题之后，顺手给第 14 题选出 A 选项。其他干扰选项统统不用考虑。

Question 15

The "social psychologists" mentioned in paragraph 2 (lines 17–34) would likely describe the "deadweight loss" phenomenon as

A) predictable.

B) questionable.

C) disturbing.

D) unprecedented.

1. 答案

A) 可预测的。

2. 精讲

细读题。

原文第 17–34 行就是完整的第 2 自然段，我们首先需要在该段中定位出 social psychologists（社会心理学家）和 deadweight loss（无谓损失）这两个词组，然后在阅读原文时牢记：本题考查的焦点是社会心理学家对 deadweight loss 的态度。

阅读第 2 段时我们发现本段出现了三种人，分别有三种不同的态度。

anthropologists（人类学家）认为送礼是 positive social process（积极的社会进步）。

但是，economists（经济学家）觉得 less favorable view（不那么喜欢），认为送礼是 an objective waste of resources（一种客观上资源浪费），送礼者花 100 块钱买的礼物，收礼者自己买可能只愿意花 80 块钱，这是一种经济学上的 deadweight loss（无谓损失）。

该段最后出现第三类人：social psychologists（社会心理学家）。文章说，无谓损失这件事，对社会心理学家来说，That in itself is not surprising to social psychologists（没什么好奇怪的）。研究发现人们很难从别人的角度思考等。

本题考查社会心理学家的观点，因此原文中 not surprising（不奇怪），很正常，对应 A 选项 predictable（意料之中的，可预测的）。

本题易错选 B 选项。如果本题考查经济学家的观点，我们才可以选择 B 选项 questionable（有问题的），经济学家确实认为 deadweight loss 是一种资源浪费，有问题。

另外两个干扰选项 C) disturbing（令人烦恼的），D) unprecedented（没有先例的）可排除。

Question 16

The passage indicates that the assumption made by gift-givers in lines 41–44 may be

A) insincere.

B) unreasonable.

C) incorrect.

D) substantiated.

1. 答案

C) 不正确的。

Question 17

Which choice provides the best evidence for the answer to the previous question?

A) Lines 53–55 ("Perhaps... consideration")

B) Lines 55–60 ("According... relationship")

C) Lines 62–65 ("As... consideration")

D) Lines 75–78 ("In... relations")

1. 答案

C)

2. 精讲

细读题和引证题组合。

这组题的难度较大，看似考查句子，实际上考查的是两个自然段的逻辑关系。

第 16 题按题目指引读第 41-44 行，文中讲到一个心理学 explanation（解释）：送礼者认为礼物越贵，收礼者越 appreciation（感激）。

注意到 16 题题干中也把这个 explanation 改写为 assumption（假定、假设），那是因为在原文第 44 行之后的句子中，已经把这个 explanation 进行了同义替换，既写成了 a link，也写成了 assumption。

这时候，大家很容易把第 16 题定位到原文第 47 行：such an assumption may be unfounded（没有根据的）。这样，大家就容易在选项 B) unreasonable（不合理的），和选项 C) incorrect（不正确的）之间犹豫，或者最终错选了 B。

但是，不管你最终选了哪个选项，当你往下做第 17 题寻证时，马上会发现第 17 题给出的四个选项全部指向第 51 行之后，也就是下一个自然段。你要立刻惊醒：原来第 16 题的出处不是第 47 行这句话，虽然这句话中包含了 assumption 一词。

赶紧先把第 16 题的答案擦掉，不管你选的是什么！仔细读完下一自然段再说！

下一段首句：Why do gift-givers assume that...（为什么送礼者假设……）

通过这句设问，我们知道了这两个自然段之间的关系：上一个自然段讲到了一个 assumption，接下来的这个自然段讲 why（为什么）送礼者做出这个假设，以及对这个假设的最终评价。

原文第 53-62 行解释了这个 assumption 的 reason：送礼者认为礼物是一个象征、一个信号；礼物越贵重，传递的信号越强（stronger signal）。

但第 62-63 行的句子说：As for gift-recipients（对收礼人来说），他们可能不是这么想。

所以，综合这些信息，大家知道了："礼物越贵，收礼者越感激"——这个假设在送礼者一方是 reasonable 的，但是对收礼者来说并非如此。

因此，我们可以说：This assumption sounds reasonable, but it is incorrect.

所以，第 16 题答案不能选 reasonable，只能选 incorrect。

第 17 题答案也即可选出 C。

这个组合题虽然难度较大，需要花时间仔细阅读两个段落，但做完之后对后面第 18 和 19 题帮助很大。

Question 18

As it is used in line 54, "convey" most nearly means

A) transport.

B) counteract.

C) exchange.

D) communicate.

---

1. 答案

D) 沟通，传达，传递。

2. 精讲

词义题。

从原文 bigger gifts convey stronger signals of thoughtfulness and consideration 我们猜得到 convey 在这里是 "传递、传达、代表" 的意思。相当于 send, represent，而且 send signal 的搭配表达在原文第 61–62 行出现过。

干扰选项中 A) transport 一词最具有迷惑性，但 transport 更强调 physically move something（事物的物理移动）。B 选项 counteract（抵消、抵抗）和 C 选项 exchange（互换）强调双方，可轻松排除。

Question 19

The authors refer to work by Camerer and others (line 56) in order to

A) offer an explanation.

B) introduce an argument.

C) question a motive.

D) support a conclusion.

---

1. 答案

A) 提供一个解释。

2. 精讲

分析目的题。

为了做第 16、17 题，我们已经读了这个自然段，已经注意到了该段首句是 Why 开始的设问。

因此接下来出现的内容信息，包括提及 Camerer，必然都是对 Why 的回答，是给出 reason，给出 explanation。

通过句子与句子间的逻辑关系，轻松搞定这一修辞题。

Question 20

The graph following the passage offers evidence that gift-givers base their predictions of how much a gift will be appreciated on

A) the appreciation level of the gift-recipients.

B) the monetary value of the gift.

C) their own desires for the gifts they purchase.

D)   their relationship with the gift-recipients.

1. 答案

B) 礼物的金钱价值。

2. 精讲

分析数据信息题。

本题考查读图能力。表头是送礼者认为的和收礼者实际的感激程度。我们看到左边第一组柱子，显然 giver（送礼者）认为：贵重的礼物（浅色柱子）带来的感激程度，要高于便宜的礼物（深色柱子）。换句话说，送礼者认为礼物带来的感激程度和礼物的价值成正比。B 选项中 monetary value（金钱价值）对应了图表中的 expensive。

BTW，虽然没有出题，但有趣的是第二组柱子告诉大家：对收礼者来说，礼物越贵，反倒感激程度越低！好有趣的结论！

做完这道题之后，大家买礼物从此不花冤枉钱！

Question 21

The authors would likely attribute the differences in gift-giver and recipient mean appreciation as represented in the graph to

A) an inability to shift perspective.

B) an increasingly materialistic culture.

C) a growing opposition to gift-giving.

D) a misunderstanding of intentions.

1. 答案

A) 难以转变思考角度。

2. 精讲

分析数据信息题。

题目问：图中送礼者和收礼者的 mean appreciation（平均感激程度）差异是什么导致的？

看似一个图表和文章信息的综合题，其实题干中去掉 as represented in the graph 这几个词，没有任何影响。

这道题实质上考查了全文的中心。

在第 31–32 行：Research has found that people often struggle to take account of others' perspective.（研究发现人们很少从别人的角度出发考虑。）这句话已经揭示了原因。

当然，最后一段进行了重申和总结。第67–68行：unable to account for the other party's perspective（不能站到对方角度）；第72–74行：they often struggle to transfer information gained from one role and apply it in another, complementary role.（他们很难将从一个角色中获得的信息运用到另一个互补的角色中。）

原文中这几处信息都在强调导致差异的根本原因：没有换位思考。

干扰选项 B) 日益增长的物质文化；C) 对送礼越来越多的反对；D) 对意图的误解；均可轻松排除。

★ 参考译文

本篇改编自 2008 年发表的 Francis J. Flynn 和 Gabrielle S. Adams 的《金钱买不到爱情：对于礼物的价格与其受欢迎程度的片面理解》。

每一天，数百万的购物者涌进商店 —— 既包括线上购物也包括去实体店购物 —— 疯狂地寻找完美的礼品。去年，美国人仅在 12 月一个月就在零售商店消费了 300 亿美元。除了购买节日礼品，绝大部分的人每年会定期在其他特定日子购买礼物，包括：婚礼、生日、结婚纪念日、毕业和孩子洗礼日。这种频繁送礼品的经历会让送礼者产生一种矛盾心理。很多人非常喜欢这种买礼物的机会，因为送礼是帮助他们和一些最亲近的人建立更紧密联系的有力手段。同时，很多人对于买礼品感到恐惧，他们担心自己买的礼物非但不能取悦他们想要送礼的对象，反而会使这些收礼者失望。

人类学家将送礼这种行为视为一种积极的社会行为，送礼会产生政治上、宗教上甚至精神上的正面作用。然而，经济学家对此的态度较为负面。1993 年 Waldfogel 指出，送礼实际上就是一种客观上的资源浪费。人们经常购买的礼物是他们的送礼对象通常不会购买，或者至少不会花那么多钱去购买的（这种现象被称作"圣诞节的无谓损失"）。送礼者可能会花费 100 美元去购买一个收礼者自己只会花 80 美元去购买的礼物。这种"无谓损失"表明送礼者根本不擅长去揣测别人喜欢什么样的礼物。而社会心理学家对于这种现象根本不感到惊讶。研究发现人们经常无法从别人的视角去考虑——他们的思考角度常常受到自我中心主义、社会预测和多重属性误差的影响。

令人感到吃惊的是，尽管送礼者往往经常送礼、收礼，但是每当他们去购买一个有意义的礼物时，他们总是倾向于过度消费。在目前的研究中，我们对于这种过量消费的问题提出了一种独一无二的心理学解释，即送礼者将他们购礼花费金额的多少与收礼者对礼物的喜爱程度等同起来（他们认为送的礼物越贵收礼者越喜欢）。尽管礼物的价格与收礼者对礼物的欣赏程度之间的联系对于送礼物者来说很有可能只是一种直觉，但这种直觉可能是毫无依据的。事实上，我们认为收礼者不太会像送礼者想的那样把他们对礼物的喜欢程度建立在礼物的贵重程度上。

为什么送礼者会认为礼品的价格与收礼者是否满意是紧密相关的呢？或许，送礼者认为礼物越贵重（比如价格越高）就会让别人觉得他们越有诚意，也越体贴。Camerer 和其他一些研究者在 1988 年曾指出，送礼物只有一种象征意义，在这个过程中送礼者尝试向收礼者传达出他们的积极态度并展示出他们愿意在未来的关系中投入资源的意图。从这种意义上来讲，为了给收礼者传达一个更为强大的信号，送礼者有可能在礼物上花更多的钱。而对于收礼者来说，他们有可能并不将更贵的礼物视作送礼者有诚意、贴心的体现，反之亦然。

因为人们在每一天甚至是同一天的不同情况下也经常在送礼者和收礼者的角色之间轮换，所以，送礼方与收礼方都无法从对方的视角去思考问题的这样一种现象似乎让人极其困惑。然而，尽管人们对于送礼者和收礼者两种角色拥有丰富的经验，但是他们经常很难将从一方角色（送礼者）中获得的经验和信息运用到另一方角色（收礼者）中去。从理论上说，在互相转换的过程中，人们无法利用从他们自己的偏好和经历中获取的信息去创造出高效的结果。从实际的角度来讲，人们每年用于购买礼物的花费高达数百美元，但是他们却从未依靠他们自己的个人经验去学会如何使他们在礼物上的花销更合理。

下面，大家一起学习《新 SAT 官方指南》Test 1 reading passage 4。建议自己先做一遍，再学习后面的真经派解析，以获得提高。

三、真经精讲 2

剧透花絮:

本文节选自英国女作家弗吉尼亚·伍尔芙（Virginia Woolf）的随笔，《三个畿尼》（*Three Guineas*）。

伍尔芙的文笔很有画面感，这篇随笔读来如同演讲稿一般，让你身临其境，仿佛也置身在泰晤士河的桥头，看到一位风姿绰约的女士，正迎着朝阳面朝人群侃侃而谈……

她是女性主义先锋，曾问："为什么男人饮酒，女人只能喝水？"

她是西方现代文学的重要先驱，很多作品至今长销不衰；但同时，她童年不幸，一生饱受精神疾病的折磨，最后投河自尽。

斯人已逝，风采永存。

Questions 32–41 are based on the following passage.

This passage is adapted from Virginia Woolf, *Three Guineas*. ©1938 by Harcourt, Inc. Here, Woolf considers the situation of women in English society.

Line　Close at hand is a bridge over the River Thames, an admirable vantage ground for us to make a survey. The river flows beneath; barges pass, laden with timber, bursting with corn; there on one side are
5　the domes and spires of the city; on the other, Westminster and the Houses of Parliament. It is a place to stand on by the hour, dreaming. But not now. Now we are pressed for time. Now we are here to consider facts; now we must fix our eyes upon the
10　procession—the procession of the sons of educated men.

　　There they go, our brothers who have been educated at public schools and universities, mounting those steps, passing in and out of those
15　doors, ascending those pulpits, preaching, teaching, administering justice, practising medicine, transacting business, making money. It is a solemn sight always—a procession, like a caravanserai crossing a desert… But now, for the past twenty
20　years or so, it is no longer a sight merely, a photograph, or fresco scrawled upon the walls of time, at which we can look with merely an esthetic appreciation. For there, trapesing along at the tail end of the procession, we go ourselves. And that
25　makes a difference. We who have looked so long at the pageant in books, or from a curtained window watched educated men leaving the house at about nine-thirty to go to an office, returning to the house at about six-thirty from an office, need look passively
30　no longer. We too can leave the house, can mount those steps, pass in and out of those doors, …make money, administer justice… We who now agitate these humble pens may in another century or two speak from a pulpit. Nobody will dare contradict us
35　then; we shall be the mouthpieces of the divine spirit—a solemn thought, is it not? Who can say whether, as time goes on, we may not dress in military uniform, with gold lace on our breasts, swords at our sides, and something like the old
40　family coal-scuttle on our heads, save that that venerable object was never decorated with plumes of white horsehair. You laugh—indeed the shadow of the private house still makes those dresses look a little queer. We have worn private clothes so
45　long… But we have not come here to laugh, or to talk of fashions—men's and women's. We are here, on the bridge, to ask ourselves certain questions. And they are very important questions; and we have very little time in which to answer them. The
50　questions that we have to ask and to answer about that procession during this moment of transition are so important that they may well change the lives of all men and women for ever. For we have to ask ourselves, here and now, do we wish to join that

55 procession, or don't we? On what terms shall we join
    that procession? Above all, where is it leading us, the
    procession of educated men? The moment is short;
    it may last five years; ten years, or perhaps only
    a matter of a few months longer… But, you will
60 object, you have no time to think; you have your
    battles to fight, your rent to pay, your bazaars to
    organize. That excuse shall not serve you, Madam.
    As you know from your own experience, and there
    are facts that prove it, the daughters of educated men
65 have always done their thinking from hand to
    mouth; not under green lamps at study tables in the
    cloisters of secluded colleges. They have thought
    while they stirred the pot, while they rocked the
    cradle. It was thus that they won us the right to our
70 brand-new sixpence. It falls to us now to go on
    thinking: how are we to spend that sixpence? Think
    we must. Let us think in offices; in omnibuses; while
    we are standing in the crowd watching Coronations
    and Lord Mayor's Shows; let us think. …in the
75 gallery of the House of Commons; in the Law
    Courts; let us think at baptisms and marriages and
    funerals. Let us never cease from thinking—what is
    this "civilization" in which we find ourselves? What
    are these ceremonies and why should we take part in
80 them? What are these professions and why
    should we make money out of them? Where in
    short is it leading us, the procession of the sons of
    educated men?

32

The main purpose of the passage is to
A) emphasize the value of a tradition.
B) stress the urgency of an issue.
C) highlight the severity of social divisions.
D) question the feasibility of an undertaking.

33

The central claim of the passage is that
A) educated women face a decision about
   how to engage with existing institutions.
B) women can have positions of influence
   in English society only if they give up
   some of their traditional roles.
C) the male monopoly on power in English
   society has had grave and continuing
   effects.
D) the entry of educated women into
   positions of power traditionally held
   by men will transform those positions.

34

Woolf uses the word "we" throughout the passage mainly to

A) reflect the growing friendliness among a group of people.

B) advance the need for candor among a group of people.

C) establish a sense of solidarity among a group of people.

D) reinforce the need for respect among a group of people.

35

According to the passage, Woolf chooses the setting of the bridge because it

A) is conducive to a mood of fanciful reflection.

B) provides a good view of the procession of the sons of educated men.

C) is within sight of historic episodes to which she alludes.

D) is symbolic of the legacy of past and present sons of educated men.

36

Woolf indicates that the procession she describes in the passage

A) has come to have more practical influence in recent years.

B) has become a celebrated feature of English public life.

C) includes all of the richest and most powerful men in England.

D) has become less exclusionary in its membership in recent years.

37

Which choice provides the best evidence for the answer to the previous question?

A) Lines 12–17 ("There…money")

B) Lines 17–19 ("It…desert")

C) Lines 23–24 ("For…ourselves")

D) Lines 30–34 ("We…pulpit")

38

Woolf characterizes the questions in lines 53–57 ("For we… men") as both

A) controversial and threatening.

B) weighty and unanswerable.

C) momentous and pressing.

D) provocative and mysterious.

39

Which choice provides the best evidence for the answer to the previous question?

A) Lines 46–47 ("We… questions")

B) Lines 48–49 ("And… them")

C) Line 57 ("The moment… short")

D) Line 62 ("That… Madam")

40

Which choice most closely captures the meaning of the figurative "sixpence" referred to in lines 70 and 71?

A) Tolerance

B) Knowledge

C) Opportunity

D) Perspective

41

The range of places and occasions listed in lines 72–77 ("Let us… funerals") mainly serves to emphasize how

A) novel the challenge faced by women is.

B) pervasive the need for critical reflection is.

C) complex the political and social issues of the day are.

D) enjoyable the career possibilities for women are.

★ 真经派精讲

Question 33

The central claim of the passage is that

A) educated women face a decision about how to engage with existing institutions.

B) women can have positions of influence in English society only if they give up some of their traditional roles.

C) the male monopoly on power in English society has had grave and continuing effects.

D) the entry of educated women into positions of power traditionally held by men will transform those positions.

1. 答案

A) 受过教育的女性面临一个应该如何参与现有制度的决定。

2. 精讲

分析论点题。题目考查全文中心论点（central claim）、全文中心思想，可以留到最后做。

首先，文章前的导语很重要，它揭示了这篇文章是作者 considers the situation of women in English society，是关于女性社会地位状态的文章，而且注意到是 1938 年发表的。大家可以大致猜到那个年代女性的社会地位肯定不高，不如现在。如果大家忽视了这个线索，整篇文章读完会满头雾水。

然后，大家看到全文只有两个自然段，逻辑结构不明显，行文的推进线索也不好把握。第一段是通过对一处景色的描述来引起下文，那么大家来重点考查第二段的逻辑结构。

第二段很长，其实是通过三个 but 的转折来推动行文逻辑。

第 19 行，第一个 but 出现，表达：但是现在，男性做的很多事，女性也可以做了。

第 45 行，第二个 but 出现，表达：但是现在，我们女性要问自己一些重要的问题，我们愿不愿意参与那个队列 that procession（指代社会主流），如何参与等。

第 59 行，第三个 but 出现，表达：女性必须继续思考，深入思考。

从第二个 but 开始，作者抛出了很多问题，大家看到文章中出现了很多问号，第三个 but 后，think 一词重复了八次。显然，作者经过前文的铺垫之后，亮出了本文中心论点：鼓励推动女性主动积极地思考，如何参与社会主流、参与社会发展建设。

作者没有给出这些问题的相应的答案，这篇演讲的目的就是推动女性去思考一些重要问题。

对全文中心有了以上理解之后，我们最后再来考查四个选项。

注意到 A 选项中的 face a decision 和 how 对应第二段后面那一连串问号；engage（参与）一词对应文中第 54 和 55 行反复出现的 join 一词以及第 79 行的 take part in（参与）。

B 选项中 give up some of their traditional roles（女性放弃传统角色），原文没有提及。

C 选项中 grave and continuing effects（男性的重大和持续影响），不是全文中心论点。

D 选项中 transform those positions（改变那些职位），原文没有提及。

Question 34

Woolf uses the word "we" throughout the passage mainly to

A) reflect the growing friendliness among a group of people.

B) advance the need for candor among a group of people.

C) establish a sense of solidarity among a group of people.

D) reinforce the need for respect among a group of people.

1. 答案

C) 在一群人中建立一种团结感。

2. 精讲

分析选词题。

该题不难。回忆一下,电影里很多激动人心的演讲中,演讲者都用"我们",很少用"你们"。

用"你们",从心理暗示上就把演讲者自己和听众天然区分开来,很难引起共鸣。

使用"我们",令人感觉演讲者和听众在地位、立场、利益、感受上都是一体的,说出的话、提出的观点更容易让听众接受。

本文中作者使用的 we,强调自己是 the educated women(受过教育的女性)中的一分子。

所以,选出 C 选项,establish a sense of solidarity(建立团结感)。

通过这道题,我们也应该牢记这一演讲技巧。

干扰选项中,friendliness(友谊)、candor(坦白)、respect(尊重),都不是使用"我们"一词的目的。

Question 35

According to the passage, Woolf chooses the setting of the bridge because it

A) is conducive to a mood of fanciful reflection.

B) provides a good view of the procession of the sons of educated men.

C) is within sight of historic episodes to which she alludes.

D) is symbolic of the legacy of past and present sons of educated men.

1. 答案

B) 提供一个良好的视野观看受过教育的男性的儿子们的队列。

2. 精讲

关系题。

注意到题干中 because 一词，可知本题考查因果关系，问为什么作者选择桥的场景。

本题较难，原文中因果关系并不明显，要理解上下文和文章逻辑推进的巧妙设计。

文章开始写景，然后写景中有一群忙碌的男人。然后第二段渐渐开始引发本文论点：女性也可以像那群男人一样参与社会，女性要思考如何参与。

就像电影镜头叙事一样，开始是一座桥的远景，桥下的船，桥旁的建筑。然后镜头逐渐拉近，聚焦到桥上人物的特写。

原文第 9–11 行，now we must fix our eyes upon the procession—the procession of the sons of educated men. 这句话就是由景转到人的镜头过渡。

因此，写景的目的是带出景中人。选出 C 选项。

Question 36

Woolf indicates that the procession she describes in the passage

A) has come to have more practical influence in recent years.

B) has become a celebrated feature of English public life.

C) includes all of the richest and most powerful men in England.

D) has become less exclusionary in its membership in recent years.

1. 答案

D) 最近几年在成员身份中的排他性变少。

Question 37

Which choice provides the best evidence for the answer to the previous question?

A) Lines 12–17 ("There… money")

B) Lines 17–19 ("It… desert")

C) Lines 23–24 ("For… ourselves")

D) Lines 30–34 ("We… pulpit")

1. 答案

C)

2. 精讲

细读题和引证题组合。

第 36 题其实考查了本文中第一个分论点，也就是第一个 but 后的观点。

第二段前面讲到了 procession（队列）中受过教育的男性在做这些事。But 之后讲，在过去的二十年，女性不再只是旁观，而是也参与了进来，这个队列里也有我们的身影。For there, trapesing along at the tail end of the procession, we go ourselves.

注意 D 选项中的 exclusionary（排他性的，独占的）一词，less exclusionary in its membership 指队列中成员的多元化，对应原文中强调女性的参与。

干扰选项中 A 选项里的比较级 more practical influence 原文没有提及；C 选项中的 the richest and most powerful 原文没有提及；B 选项易误选，因为队列中各种人的工作职业确实是社会生活的一个缩影和比喻，但原文并没提及这是英国社会区别于其他国家的 celebrated feature（显著特征）。

第 37 题顺带选出 C 选项。

Question 38

Woolf characterizes the questions in lines 53–57 ("For we… men") as both

A) controversial and threatening.

B) weighty and unanswerable.

C) momentous and pressing.

D) provocative and mysterious.

1. 答案

C) 重要和紧迫。

Question 39

Which choice provides the best evidence for the answer to the previous question?

A Lines 46–47 ("We… questions")

B) Lines 48–49 ("And… them")

C) Line 57 ("The moment… short")

D) Line 62 ("That… Madam")

1. 答案

B)

2. 精讲

这又是一个细读题和引证题组合。

第 38 题定位清晰，问作者对第 53–57 行这些问题的特点定义。显然要求大家读第 53 行之前或第 57 行之后，通过上下文阅读去寻找。

第 48–49 行：And they are very important questions; and we have little time in which to answer them. 显然，这些问题的特点有两个：very important（重要）和 little time to answer（紧迫）。

选出 C 选项，momentous（重要的）and pressing（紧迫的）。

注意 B 选项有干扰性，weighty（重要的）正确，unanswerable（无解的）错误。

第 39 题选出 B 选项。

Question 40

Which choice most closely captures the meaning of the figurative "sixpence" referred to in lines 70 and 71?

A) Tolerance

B) Knowledge

C) Opportunity

D) Perspective

---

1. 答案

C）机会。

2. 精讲

词义题。

虽然题干问法不同，问 sixpence（六便士硬币）一词的 figurative（比喻的）含义，

但该题本质上是一个词义题。

回到原文第 70 行和 71 行：她们为我们赢得了这个崭新 ×× 的权利；我们应该如何花费利用这个 ××？

分别将四个选项 tolerance（宽容）、knowledge（知识）、opportunity（机会）、perspective（态度）代入原文 ×× 理解。

显然，C 选项贴切。

Question 41

The range of places and occasions listed in lines 72–77 ("Let us… funerals") mainly serves to emphasize how

A) novel the challenge faced by women is.

B) pervasive the need for critical reflection is.

C) complex the political and social issues of the day are.

D) enjoyable the career possibilities for women are.

---

1. 答案

B) 重要反思的需求的广泛性。

2. 精讲

分析目的题。

原文第 72–77 行用了排比的修辞手法，罗列出在办公室里、公交车上，在人群中、法院里，在洗礼、婚礼、葬礼上，都需要思考。题目考查作者通过这一系列排比想要强调什么，以及这一修辞手法的目的。

显然，罗列这么多场景，是为了强调这种重要思考的广泛性，大家应该随时随地去思考这些重要问题。

对应 B 选项：(how) pervasive（广泛的）the need for critical reflection（重要反思）is。

其他三个干扰选项为：A) 女性面临挑战的崭新性；C) 每天政治和社会问题的复杂性；D) 女性职业可能的乐趣性。

⭐ 参考译文

本文改编自 1938 年发表的 Virginia Woolf 的《三个畿尼》。在本文中，Wolf 讨论了英国社会中女性所处的地位。

一座横跨泰晤士河的桥看起来触手可及。这里是一个上佳的场所，便于我们好好地观察一番。河水从桥下流过，驳船穿过时可以看到它们装满了木材或谷子；视线的一边可以看到城市建筑物的穹顶与尖顶，另一边则可以看到威斯敏斯特和议会大厦。这里是一个可以驻足很久的地方，使人思绪联翩。但是，现在可不是时候。现在我们时间紧迫。现在我们在这里必须考虑的是眼前的事实；我们现在必须将我们的目光聚焦在眼前的人群队列上——这是由那些受过教育的男性的儿子们排成的队列。

他们来了，这些在公立学校和大学受教育的我们的兄弟们。他们迈上台阶，不断地穿过那些门，走入他们的各种岗位：布道，授课，执法，行医，做生意，赚钱。这种场面总是很神圣，一个队列，就像横穿沙漠的大商队。但是现在，在过去的二十年甚至更久的时间里，它不再仅仅是一幅场景、一张照片，或是沿着时间的墙所铺开的壁画，因为这样的话我们只能从视觉审美的角度对它加以鉴赏。站在这里，沿着队列的尾迹，我们自己也加入其中。这大有不同。一直以来只能从书本中了解盛典游行或是透过窗户观察那些受教育的男性在早上九点半离开家去办公室、在下午六点半从办公室回家的我们不再被动地旁观了。我们也能离开家，迈上台阶，穿过那些门，去赚钱，去执法。现在我们拿着自己手中的笔，再过一两个世纪，我们也可以在讲台上演讲。那时没有人敢于质疑我们，我们会成为神圣灵魂的代言人。这是一个严肃的想法，不是吗？谁敢说随着时间的推移，我们就不会穿上军装？我们的胸前不会装饰有金色的花边？我们的腰上不会佩上宝剑？我们的头上不会出现像旧式家用煤斗一样的军帽？只不过那个神圣的东西绝不能用白马的鬃毛装饰。你一定会笑。事实上，在居家房子的阴影中穿上这些衣服仍然会使得我们看上去有一丝古怪。我们穿着那些居家的衣服已经太久了……但是，我们不是来谈笑或是来讨论男性和女性的时尚的。我们聚集在桥上是为了自我思考某些问题，它们是一些重要的问题，我们须在有限的时间内找到答案。处于这样一个巨大转折的时刻，关于"队列"的问题是如此的重要，我们必须要提问并得出答案，这些答案重要到可能会永远地改变所有男性和女性的生活。此时此刻，我们必须扪心自问：我们是否愿意加入那个"队列"？要满足什么样的条件我们才能加入这个"队列"？最重要的是，这个受过教育的男性的"队列"将把我们引向何方？这段时期很短暂，它有可能持续五年，十年，或许只是几个月的事……但是，你可能会反对，认为你没有没时间去思考这个问题；你有你自己的事情要处理，你有房租要付，还有自己的生意要经营。女士，这种借口可不是每次都管用。生活经验让你明白，并且大量事实也能证明，受过教育的男性的女儿就算生活艰难也会时常思考；她们不是坐在大学课桌前借着台灯思考，而是一边做饭一边思考，一边晃着摇篮一边思考。正是这样，她们才帮助我们赢得了获得崭新机会的权利。现在轮到我们继续思考：我们该如何去利用这次机会呢？是的，我们必须继续思考；让我们在办公室里思考，在公交车里思考，在站在拥挤的人群中观看加冕礼和伦敦市长游行的时候思考；让我们思考吧……在下议院的大厅里，在法院里，在洗礼、婚礼和葬礼上思考。让我们永远不要停止思考——那些可以帮助我们找到自我的文明到底是什么？这些形形色色的活动和仪式到底是什么？我们为什么要参与其中？这些职业是什么？为什么我们要从这些职业中赚钱？那些受过教育的男性的儿子们所从事的职业将把我们引向何方呢？

第七章

科技类文章真题精讲

一、总论

科技类文章是大家最熟悉的一类阅读文章，它是各种英语阅读考试中当之无愧的明星主演。

科技类文章大多取材自国外著名的科普杂志或论文，向全社会传递前沿新知，所以不要求读者具有相应的专业背景。SAT 阅读的科技类文章一共两篇，或者一篇加上双短文，主要涉及地球科学、生物、化学、物理等领域。

要阐明一种新的概念、观点、发现、方法，并让读者理解接受，通常会用到两种方式：提供*事实论据*（实验结果、统计数据、观察记录等）或*理论论据*（普遍承认的道理或逻辑推理），也就是我们经常说的摆事实、讲道理。

把握住科技类文章的*论点*、*论据*和*论证方式*这三点，文章的脉络就清晰了。

★ 文章特点

● 中心明确，文章结构清晰（没有文学文章里的倒叙、补叙、插叙等）。

● 词汇专业性强，句式严谨，长难句多，语言具有逻辑性。

★ 技巧真经

● 不要受专业术语的影响，心中用一个字母代替。

● 读到表达观点的中心句随时在下面画线。

● 科技文章自然段之间的逻辑关系很清晰（总分、并列、递进、转折、因果、解释等），要尽量理解是哪一种。

● 新观点、新发现通常会颠覆你的认知，要敢于接受，不能固守自己原有的背景知识去解题。

下面，大家一起来学习《新 SAT 官方指南》Test 1 reading passage 3。建议自己先做一遍，然后再学习后面的真经派解析，以获得提高。

二、真题精讲 1

剧透花絮：

下面这篇文章的作者是两位诺贝尔奖得主，沃森（J. D. Watson）和克里克（F. H. C. Crick）。他们在 1953 年发现了 DNA 双螺旋的结构，打开了"生命之谜"。

从此，分子遗传学、分子免疫学、细胞生物学等新学科如雨后春笋般出现；基因筛查、靶向治疗等应用让每个人受益；现代基因工程甚至瞄着提升人类寿命、实现长生不老的终极目标。

"仙人抚我顶，结发授长生。"

让我们认真阅读这两位仙人、大神写的论文，向他们致敬。

"这个领域里的杰出科学家花费毕生心血得到的研究结论、智慧结晶，难道不值得我们尊重珍惜，静心阅读吗？"

这句话是我对学为贵集团的"贵粉儿"们说的，也送给你。

Questions 22–31 are based on the following passage and supplementary material.

This passage is adapted from J. D. Watson and F. H. C. Crick, "Genetical Implications of the Structure of Deoxyribonucleic Acid." ©1953 by *Nature* Publishing Group. Watson and Crick deduced the structure of DNA using evidence from Rosalind Franklin and R. G. Gosling's X-ray crystallography diagrams of DNA and from Erwin Chargaff's data on the base composition of DNA.

Line

The chemical formula of deoxyribonucleic acid (DNA) is now well established. The molecule is a very long chain, the backbone of which consists of a regular alternation of sugar and phosphate groups.

5 To each sugar is attached a nitrogenous base, which can be of four different types. Two of the possible bases—adenine and guanine—are purines, and the other two—thymine and cytosine—are pyrimidines. So far as is known, the sequence of bases along the

10 chain is irregular. The monomer unit, consisting of phosphate, sugar and base, is known as a nucleotide.

The first feature of our structure which is of biological interest is that it consists not of one chain, but of two. These two chains are both coiled around

15 a common fiber axis. It has often been assumed that since there was only one chain in the chemical formula there would only be one in the structural unit. However, the density, taken with the X-ray evidence, suggests very strongly that there are two.

20 The other biologically important feature is the manner in which the two chains are held together. This is done by hydrogen bonds between the bases. The bases are joined together in pairs, a single base from one chain being hydrogen-bonded to a single

25 base from the other. The important point is that only certain pairs of bases will fit into the structure. One member of a pair must be a purine and the other a pyrimidine in order to bridge between the two chains. If a pair consisted of two purines, for

30 example, there would not be room for it.

We believe that the bases will be present almost entirely in their most probable forms. If this is true, the conditions for forming hydrogen bonds are more restrictive, and the only pairs of bases possible are:

35 adenine with thymine, and guanine with cytosine. Adenine, for example, can occur on either chain; but when it does, its partner on the other chain must always be thymine.

The phosphate-sugar backbone of our model is

40 completely regular, but any sequence of the pairs of bases can fit into the structure. It follows that in a long molecule many different permutations are possible, and it therefore seems likely that the precise sequence of bases is the code which carries the

45 genetical information. If the actual order of the bases on one of the pair of chains were given, one could write down the exact order of the bases on the other one, because of the specific pairing. Thus one chain is, as it were, the complement of the other, and it is

50 this feature which suggests how the deoxyribonucleic acid molecule might duplicate itself.

The table shows, for various organisms, the percentage of each of the four types of nitrogenous bases in that organism's DNA.

Base Composition of DNA				
Organism	Percentage of base in organism's DNA			
	adenine (%)	guanine (%)	cytosine (%)	thymine (%)
Maize	26.8	22.8	23.2	27.2
Octopus	33.2	17.6	17.6	31.6
Chicken	28.0	22.0	21.6	28.4
Rat	28.6	21.4	20.5	28.4
Human	29.3	20.7	20.0	30.0
Grasshopper	29.3	20.5	20.7	29.3
Sea urchin	32.8	17.7	17.3	32.1
Wheat	27.3	22.7	22.8	27.1
Yeast	31.3	18.7	17.1	32.9
E. coli	24.7	26.0	25.7	23.6

Adapted from Manju Bansal, "DNA Structure: Revisiting the Watson-Crick Double Helix." ©2003 by Current Science Association, Bangalore.

22

The authors use the word "backbone" in lines 3 and 39 to indicate that

A) only very long chains of DNA can be taken from an organism with a spinal column.

B) the main structure of a chain in a DNA molecule is composed of repeating units.

C) a chain in a DNA molecule consists entirely of phosphate groups or of sugars.

D) nitrogenous bases form the main structural unit of DNA.

23

A student claims that nitrogenous bases pair randomly with one another. Which of the following statements in the passage contradicts the student's claim?

A) Lines 5–6 ("To each... types")

B) Lines 9–10 ("So far... irregular")

C) Lines 23–25 ("The bases... other")

D) Lines 27–29 ("One member... chains")

24

In the second paragraph (lines 12–19), what do the authors claim to be a feature of biological interest?

A) The chemical formula of DNA

B) The common fiber axis

C) The X-ray evidence

D) DNA consisting of two chains

25

The authors' main purpose of including the information about X-ray evidence and density is to

A) establish that DNA is the molecule that carries the genetic information.

B) present an alternate hypothesis about the composition of a nucleotide.

C) provide support for the authors' claim about the number of chains in a molecule of DNA.

D) confirm the relationship between the density of DNA and the known chemical formula of DNA.

26

Based on the passage, the authors' statement "If a pair consisted of two purines, for example, there would not be room for it" (lines 29–30) implies that a pair

A) of purines would be larger than the space between a sugar and a phosphate group.

B) of purines would be larger than a pair consisting of a purine and a pyrimidine.

C) of pyrimidines would be larger than a pair of purines.

D) consisting of a purine and a pyrimidine would be larger than a pair of pyrimidines.

27

The authors' use of the words "exact," "specific," and "complement" in lines 47–49 in the final paragraph functions mainly to

A) confirm that the nucleotide sequences are known for most molecules of DNA.

B) counter the claim that the sequences of bases along a chain can occur in any order.

C) support the claim that the phosphate-sugar backbone of the authors' model is completely regular.

D) emphasize how one chain of DNA may serve as a template to be copied during DNA replication.

28

Based on the table and passage, which choice gives the correct percentages of the purines in yeast DNA?

A) 17.1% and 18.7%

B) 17.1% and 32.9%

C) 18.7% and 31.3%

D) 31.3% and 32.9%

29

Do the data in the table support the authors' proposed pairing of bases in DNA?

A) Yes, because for each given organism, the percentage of adenine is closest to the percentage of thymine, and the percentage of guanine is closest to the percentage of cytosine.

B) Yes, because for each given organism, the percentage of adenine is closest to the percentage of guanine, and the percentage of cytosine is closest to the percentage of thymine.

C) No, because for each given organism, the percentage of adenine is closest to the percentage of thymine, and the percentage of guanine is closest to the percentage of cytosine.

D) No, because for each given organism, the percentage of adenine is closest to the percentage of guanine, and the percentage of cytosine is closest to the percentage of thymine.

30

According to the table, which of the following pairs of base percentages in sea urchin DNA provides evidence in support of the answer to the previous question?

A) 17.3% and 17.7%

B) 17.3% and 32.1%

C) 17.3% and 32.8%

D) 17.7% and 32.8%

31

Based on the table, is the percentage of adenine in each organism's DNA the same or does it vary, and which statement made by the authors is most consistent with that data?

A) The same; "Two of... pyrimidines" (lines 6–8)

B) The same; "The important... structure" (lines 25–26)

C) It varies; "Adenine... thymine" (lines 36–38)

D) It varies; "It follows... information" (lines 41–45)

⭐ **真经派精讲**

> **Question 22**
>
> The authors use the word "backbone" in lines 3 and 39 to indicate that
>
> A) only very long chains of DNA can be taken from an organism with a spinal column.
>
> B) the main structure of a chain in a DNA molecule is composed of repeating units.
>
> C) a chain in a DNA molecule consists entirely of phosphate groups or of sugars.
>
> D) nitrogenous bases form the main structural unit of DNA.

1. 答案

B) 在一个 DNA 分子中的一个链的主要结构是由重复单元构成。

2. 精讲

分析选词题。

首先，backbone 一词指"背后的骨头"，那自然就是"脊柱、脊梁"了；但该词还有一个常见的引申含义"基础、支柱"。

原文第 3 行中，which 指代前面的 a very long chain；consists of 对应 B 选项中的 is composed of；regular alternation（有规律的交替）对应 B 选项中的 repeating（重复）；sugar and phosphate groups 对应 B 选项中的 units。

同时，原文第 40 行也重复出现了 regular 一词，B 选项中 repeating 得到了再一次确认。所以，可以看出原文中 backbone 一词使用了其引申义"基础、支柱"，对应 B 选项中的 the main structure。

干扰选项 A 的设计很有意思，spinal column（脊柱）是对 backbone 的直译。这一选项显然专坑那些词汇量大、但阅读水平不好的考生。你没选 A，估计是因为词汇量小，不认识 spinal（脊柱的）一词，反而因祸得福，哈哈。

C 选项中的 or 和原文中的 and 矛盾；D 选项说是 nitrogenous bases 构成了 DNA 的主要结构单元。这一表述错误，原文中说的是 sugar and phosphate groups。

Question 23

A student claims that nitrogenous bases pair randomly with one another. Which of the following statements in the passage contradicts the student's claim?

A) Lines 5–6 ("To each... types")

B) Lines 9–10 ("So far... irregular")

C) Lines 23–25 ("The bases... other")

D) Lines 27–29 ("One member... chains")

1. 答案

D)

2. 精讲

单独出现的引证题。

可以定位题干中的 nitrogenous bases，去寻找与 pair randomly（随机组队）contradicts（相矛盾）的反义词表达。

三个干扰选项对应的原文确实都谈及 nitrogenous bases 的特点，但没有驳斥 pair randomly。

注意到 D 选项指示的原文第 27 行：One member of a pair must be a purine and the other (must be) a pyrimidine in order to... 这里的 must 其实就是 randomly 的反义词；句子后面的 in order to 其实是给出了 must 的原因，为什么不能 pair randomly。而且，后面 If 开始的虚拟语气句子也是在进一步解释该原因。

Question 24

In the second paragraph (lines 12–19), what do the authors claim to be a feature of biological interest?

A) The chemical formula of DNA

B) The common fiber axis

C) The X-ray evidence

D) DNA consisting of two chains

1. 答案

D) DNA 包含两条链。

2. 精讲

细读题。

该题简单，因为第二段中心句为首句，非常明确。

首句中强调了 the first feature 是 not of one chain, but of two，使用了 not...but 的强调表达。而且该段末句，通过 however 的转折，再次强调了 X-ray evidence（X 光证据）表明 there are two。

所以，two chains 就是第二段中对应 the first feature 的核心词。直接选出 D 选项。

Question 25

The authors' main purpose of including the information about X-ray evidence and density is to

A) establish that DNA is the molecule that carries the genetic information.

B) present an alternate hypothesis about the composition of a nucleotide.

C) provide support for the authors' claim about the number of chains in a molecule of DNA.

D) confirm the relationship between the density of DNA and the known chemical formula of DNA.

1. 答案

C) 为作者关于 DNA 分子中链条数量的论点提供支持。

2. 精讲

分析目的题。

如果没有上一道题（第 24 题），本题单独出现，相信难度会大很多。但由于我们刚刚做完了第 24 题，对第二段的行文结构逻辑有了判断，也知道了第二段最核心的内容是 two chains，那么第二段首句后面的所有内容其实都在解释、证明、支持（provide support）two 这个词。

本题 C 选项中 the number 对应 two，可轻松选出。

Question 26

Based on the passage, the authors' statement "If a pair consisted of two purines, for example, there would not be room for it" (lines 29–30) implies that a pair

A) of purines would be larger than the space between a sugar and a phosphate group.

B) of purines would be larger than a pair consisting of a purine and a pyrimidine.

C) of pyrimidines would be larger than a pair of purines.

D) consisting of a purine and a pyrimidine would be larger than a pair of pyrimidines.

1. 答案

B) 两个 purines 会比一个 purine 和一个 pyrimidine 配对更大。

2. 精讲

注意到题干中的 imply 一词，这是细读题中的暗示题。

同样，该题和前面的第 23 题有紧密联系。

原文第 29 行 If 开始的这个虚拟语气的句子是为了解释上一句话，为什么其中一个必须（must）是 purine，而另一个必须是 pyrimidine，才能配成一对（pair）。

如果（If）两者都是 purines，就没有空间（room）了。

显然，两个 purines，比起 purine 和 pyrimidine 配对，所占的空间更大。符合 B 选项的表达。

Question 27

The authors' use of the words "exact," "specific," and "complement" in lines 47–49 in the final paragraph functions mainly to

A) confirm that the nucleotide sequences are known for most molecules of DNA.

B) counter the claim that the sequences of bases along a chain can occur in any order.

C) support the claim that the phosphate-sugar backbone of the authors' model is completely regular.

D) emphasize how one chain of DNA may serve as a template to be copied during DNA replication.

1. 答案

D) 强调在 DNA 复制中，DNA 的一条链如何作为模板被复制。

2. 精讲

分析选词题。

先要阅读这些词所在的句子（lines 47–49），然后要搞懂作者写这些句子的目的，也就是说，更重要的是要认真阅读第 47–49 行前和后的句子，才能找到本题的解题线索。

本题的核心线索来自第 49–50 行：It is this feature which... 这个强调句型。我们学过 It is...that (who)... 是强调句型，其实 which 也是可以的。

这句话中的 this feature（这种特点）指代的是什么呢？其实就是 exact, specific, complement 这几个词所强调的特点。因为 chains 有 exact（准确）、specific（特定）、complement（相互补充）的这些特点，所以，the deoxyribonucleic acid molecule might duplicate itself（DNA 分子可以自我复制）。

我们通过理解 this feature 的指代，然后读出上下文因果关系（thus），再加上强调句型（It is this feature which...），就可以确定 D 选项了。

作者使用 exact（准确）、specific（特定）、complement（相互补充）这些词来表达 chains 的特点，而正是因为这些 features，所以它可以作为 template（模板）来 copy（复制）。

注意到 D 选项中的 copy、replication（复制）对应原文中 duplicate 一词。

本题考点设计非常丰富，有因果关系（thus）的理解，有指代关系（this feature）的理解，有强调句型的考点，还有 duplicate 和 copy、replication 的同义替换。

好的命题就像一道美味佳肴，鲜香麻辣，四种口感都有，回味无穷，你都一一体会、欣赏到了吗？

Question 28

Based on the table and passage, which choice gives the correct percentages of the purines in yeast DNA?

A) 17.1% and 18.7%

B) 17.1% and 32.9%

C) 18.7% and 31.3%

D) 31.3% and 32.9%

1. 答案

C)

2. 精讲

分析数据信息题，较简单。

注意题干中的 purines 一词，回到表格中没有找到该词，于是先需要定位原文。

原文 purines 一词最先出现在第 7 行："—adenine and guanine—are purines"，由此知道，purines 包含了 adenine 和 guanine。

再次回到表格中，定位到 yeast 的 adenine 和 guanine 的百分比，分别是 31.3 和 18.7，对应答案 C。

Question 29

Do the data in the table support the authors' proposed pairing of bases in DNA?

A) Yes, because for each given organism, the percentage of adenine is closest to the percentage of thymine, and the percentage of guanine is closest to the percentage of cytosine.

B) Yes, because for each given organism, the percentage of adenine is closest to the percentage of guanine, and the percentage of cytosine is closest to the percentage of thymine.

C) No, because for each given organism, the percentage of adenine is closest to the percentage of thymine, and the percentage of guanine is closest to the percentage of cytosine.

D) No, because for each given organism, the percentage of adenine is closest to the percentage of guanine, and the percentage of cytosine is closest to the percentage of thymine.

---

1. 答案

A) 是，因为对每一种特定的有机物，adenine 的百分比和 thymine 的百分比最接近，而且 guanine 的百分比和 cytosine 的百分比最接近。

2. 精讲

分析数据信息题。

注意到题目的问法：表格中的数据是否支持作者提出的观点？常识告诉我们，作者在文章中引用图表数据，必然是用来论证支持自己观点的。如果作者的观点和图表中的客观数据矛盾，那是作者的写作观点有问题，与数据事实不符。所以，直接先排除 C、D 选项。

阅读 A、B 选项，发现在说哪两个东西百分比最接近的问题，回到表格，看一看数据，对比一下，轻松发现 adenine 和 thymine 接近，guanine 和 cytosine 接近 [比如在 Octopus（章鱼）身体中，guanine 和 cytosine 都是 17.6%]，所以选出 A。

以上是捷径解题的方法。

如果真要找到作者观点的原文出处，可以阅读第 35 行：adenine with thymine, and guanine with cytosine，并参考上下文理解：这四个东西两两配对。有多少 adenine，就应该有多少 thymine 与之配对，所以 adenine 和 thymine 所占百分比应该接近。

Question 30

According to the table, which of the following pairs of base percentages in sea urchin DNA provides evidence in support of the answer to the previous question?

A) 17.3% and 17.7%

B) 17.3% and 32.1%

C) 17.3% and 32.8%

D) 17.7% and 32.8%

1. 答案

A)

2. 精讲

分析数据信息题。

如果上一题解题思路清晰并做对，本题就是送分题，有点像引证题。

在表格中定位 Sea urchin（海胆）的 DNA 构成，发现 32.8 和 32.1，或者 17.7 和 17.3，这两组数任何一组都符合上一题 A 选项的表达。故本题选出 A 选项。

Question 31

Based on the table, is the percentage of adenine in each organism's DNA the same or does it vary, and which statement made by the authors is most consistent with that data?

A) The same; "Two of... pyrimidines" (lines 6–8)

B) The same; "The important... structure" (lines 25–26)

C) It varies; "Adenine... thymine" (lines 36–38)

D) It varies; "It follows... information" (lines 41–45)

---

1. 答案

D)

2. 精讲

可能 SAT 命题者察觉到上一题太简单、太送分、命题太水，本题想要找补回来，于是本题设计了包括数据分析和引证在内的两个问题。

第一个问题：每种生物体内 DNA 中 adenine 的百分比一样吗？表格第二列看一眼，明显不一样（varies），有 24.7% 的，也有 33.2% 的。排除 A、B 选项。

第二个问题：原文中哪里有相关表达？分别阅读 C、D 选项所指示的原文出处，哪里在强调这种不同？

原文第 41 行开始：It follows that in a long molecule many different permutations are possible, and it therefore seems likely that the precise sequence of bases is the code which carries the genetical information.

我们注意到单词 different（不同的），注意到 genetical information（基因信息）的 code（代码）。

结合表格信息思考下：各种生物的 DNA 都是由四种东西构成，那是什么让人和章鱼的基因代码不一样？是 DNA 的四种成分的顺序（sequence）不同、百分比不同。

造物主真是神奇呀！DNA 中四种物质的不同排列组合，就形成玉米、章鱼、小鸡……还有学霸、学渣。

噢，不对。学霸和学渣的区别应该不是 DNA 造成的，而是学习习惯、学习方法、学习材料不同等因素造成的。

希望本书的读者 —— 学为贵真经派的"贵粉儿"都早日变身学霸！哈哈！

★ 参考译文

本文改编自 1953 年在《自然》杂志上发表的 J. D. Watson 和 F. H. C. Crick 的文章《脱氧核糖核酸的结构在基因学上的意义》。Watson 和 Crick 通过使用 Rosalind Franklin 和 R. G. Gosling 的 DNA 的 X 光晶体学图像和 Erwin Chargaff 的 DNA 基本组成的数据推导出

了 DNA 的结构。

现在人们已经弄清了脱氧核糖核酸（DNA）的化学组成。它的分子是一条非常长的链，这条链的核心包含了有规律地交替出现的脱氧核糖和磷酸基团。

每一个脱氧核糖都与一个含氮碱基相连，后者分为四种不同的类型。其中两种可能的含氮碱基是嘌呤——腺嘌呤和鸟嘌呤；另外两种是嘧啶——胞嘧啶和胸腺嘧啶。就目前的已知情况来看，沿着分子链出现的含氮碱基的排列顺序是不规则的。单体单元由磷酸基团、脱氧核糖和含氮碱基构成，被称作核苷酸。

DNA 结构能够引起人们生物学兴趣的首要特征是，它包含的不是一条链，而是两条。这两条链绕着一个共有的纤维轴，呈螺旋状。我们过去一直这样假设：因为在化学方程中只有一条链，所以 DNA 的结构单元中也应该只有一条链。然而，通过 X 射线得到的 DNA 的密度图清晰地表明存在着两条链。

在生物学上另外一个非常重要的特征是两条链的连接方式。它是通过碱基之间的氢键实现的。这些碱基成对地连在一起，一条链上的碱基与另一条链上的碱基通过氢键一一对应连接。重要的是，只有特定的碱基配对才能匹配到结构中去。配对的碱基一方必须是嘌呤，而另一方必须是嘧啶，这样两条链才能连接起来。例如，如果一对碱基都是嘌呤，DNA 将没有足够的空间容纳它们。

我们认为，碱基将几乎完全以它们最可能的形式存在。如果这是真的，形成氢键的形式将会更加严格，碱基配对的形式仅可能是：腺嘌呤和胸腺嘧啶，鸟嘌呤和胞嘧啶。比如说，如果一条链上出现的是腺嘌呤，此时，对应的另一条链上必须是胸腺嘧啶。

DNA 模型的脱氧核糖—磷酸基团框架是完全规律性的，但是任意顺序的碱基配对都可以适应到整个结构中去。这使得在一个长的分子中很多不同的排列成为可能。因此，碱基的准确排序可以被编码以携带基因信息似乎是有可能的。如果双链中一条链上的成对碱基的实际顺序是确定的，那么，我们就可以通过特定的配对方式写下另一条链上的碱基的准确顺序。因此，一条链其实就是另一条链的对应补充，而正是这种特征体现出脱氧核糖核酸是如何自我复制的。

下面，大家一起来学习《新 SAT 官方指南》Test 1 reading passage 5。建议自己先做一遍，再学习后面的真经派解析，以获得提高。

三、真题精讲 2

剧透花絮：

"家里有矿"是很多人的幻想。

"太空有矿"却是公认的事实，就看谁能去开采。

现在，全球已经有很多商业公司把眼光投向广袤无垠的太空。据说，有的星球遍布黄金，有的是由钻石构成。最重要的是，它们都还是无主之地。

读一读下面这两篇短文，了解先行者们雄心勃勃的计划及其风险和隐忧。

说不定将来你也会加入宇宙探险的大军之中。

年轻人，你的征途是星辰大海。

Questions 42–52 are based on the following passages.

Passage 1 is adapted from Michael Slezak, "Space Mining: the Next Gold Rush?" ©2013 by *New Scientist*. Passage 2 is from the editors of *New Scientist*, "Taming the Final Frontier." ©2013 by *New Scientist*.

Passage 1

Line Follow the money and you will end up in space. That's the message from a first-of-its-kind forum on mining beyond Earth.

Convened in Sydney by the Australian Centre for
5   Space Engineering Research, the event brought together mining companies, robotics experts, lunar scientists, and government agencies that are all working to make space mining a reality.

The forum comes hot on the heels of the
10 2012 unveiling of two private asteroid-mining firms. Planetary Resources of Washington says it will launch its first prospecting telescopes in two years, while Deep Space Industries of Virginia hopes to be harvesting metals from asteroids by 2020. Another
15 commercial venture that sprung up in 2012, Golden Spike of Colorado, will be offering trips to the moon, including to potential lunar miners.

Within a few decades, these firms may be meeting earthly demands for precious metals, such as
20 platinum and gold, and the rare earth elements vital for personal electronics, such as yttrium and lanthanum. But like the gold rush pioneers who transformed the western United States, the first space miners won't just enrich themselves. They also hope
25 to build an off-planet economy free of any bonds with Earth, in which the materials extracted and processed from the moon and asteroids are delivered for space-based projects.

In this scenario, water mined from other
30 worlds could become the most desired commodity. "In the desert, what's worth more: a kilogram of gold or a kilogram of water?" asks Kris Zacny of HoneyBee Robotics in New York. "Gold is useless. Water will let you live."

35 Water ice from the moon's poles could be sent to astronauts on the International Space Station for drinking or as a radiation shield. Splitting water into oxygen and hydrogen makes spacecraft fuel, so ice-rich asteroids could become interplanetary
40 refuelling stations.

Companies are eyeing the iron, silicon, and aluminium in lunar soil and asteroids, which could be used in 3D printers to make spare parts or machinery. Others want to turn space dirt into
45 concrete for landing pads, shelters, and roads.

Passage 2

The motivation for deep-space travel is shifting from discovery to economics. The past year has seen a flurry of proposals aimed at bringing celestial riches down to Earth. No doubt this will make a few
50 billionaires even wealthier, but we all stand to gain: the mineral bounty and spin-off technologies could enrich us all.

But before the miners start firing up their rockets, we should pause for thought. At first glance, space
55 mining seems to sidestep most environmental concerns: there is (probably!) no life on asteroids, and thus no habitats to trash. But its consequences— both here on Earth and in space—merit careful consideration.

60 Part of this is about principles. Some will argue that space's "magnificent desolation" is not ours to despoil, just as they argue that our own planet's poles should remain pristine. Others will suggest that glutting ourselves on space's riches is not an
65 acceptable alternative to developing more sustainable ways of earthly life.

History suggests that those will be hard lines to hold, and it may be difficult to persuade the public that such barren environments are worth preserving.
70 After all, they exist in vast abundance, and even fewer people will experience them than have walked through Antarctica's icy landscapes.

There's also the emerging off-world economy to consider. The resources that are valuable in orbit and
75 beyond may be very different to those we prize on Earth. Questions of their stewardship have barely been broached—and the relevant legal and regulatory framework is fragmentary, to put it mildly.

Space miners, like their earthly counterparts,
80 are often reluctant to engage with such questions. One speaker at last week's space-mining forum in Sydney, Australia, concluded with a plea that regulation should be avoided. But miners have much to gain from a broad agreement on the for-profit
85 exploitation of space. Without consensus, claims will be disputed, investments risky, and the gains made insecure. It is in all of our long-term interests to seek one out.

42

In lines 9–17, the author of Passage 1 mentions several companies primarily to

A) note the technological advances that make space mining possible.

B) provide evidence of the growing interest in space mining.

C) emphasize the large profits to be made from space mining.

D) highlight the diverse ways to carry out space mining operations.

43

The author of Passage 1 indicates that space mining could have which positive effect?

A) It could yield materials important to Earth's economy.

B) It could raise the value of some precious metals on Earth.

C) It could create unanticipated technological innovations.

D) It could change scientists' understanding of space resources.

44

Which choice provides the best evidence for the answer to the previous question?

A) Lines 18–22 ("Within... lanthanum")

B) Lines 24–28 ("They... projects")

C) Lines 29–30 ("In this... commodity")

D) Lines 41–44 ("Companies... machinery")

45

As used in line 19, "demands" most nearly means

A) offers.

B) claims.

C) inquiries.

D) desires.

46

What function does the discussion of water in lines 35–40 serve in Passage 1?

A) It continues an extended comparison that begins in the previous paragraph.

B) It provides an unexpected answer to a question raised in the previous paragraph.

C) It offers hypothetical examples supporting a claim made in the previous paragraph.

D) It examines possible outcomes of a proposal put forth in the previous paragraph.

47

The central claim of Passage 2 is that space mining has positive potential but

A) it will end up encouraging humanity's reckless treatment of the environment.

B) its effects should be thoughtfully considered before it becomes a reality.

C) such potential may not include replenishing key resources that are disappearing on Earth.

D) experts disagree about the commercial viability of the discoveries it could yield.

48

As used in line 68, "hold" most nearly means

A) maintain.

B) grip.

C) restrain.

D) withstand.

49

Which statement best describes the relationship between the passages?

A) Passage 2 refutes the central claim advanced in Passage 1.

B) Passage 2 illustrates the phenomenon described in more general terms in Passage 1.

C) Passage 2 argues against the practicality of the proposals put forth in Passage 1.

D) Passage 2 expresses reservations about developments discussed in Passage 1.

50

The author of Passage 2 would most likely respond to the discussion of the future of space mining in lines 18–28, Passage 1, by claiming that such a future

A) is inconsistent with the sustainable use of space resources.

B) will be difficult to bring about in the absence of regulations.

C) cannot be attained without technologies that do not yet exist.

D) seems certain to affect Earth's economy in a negative way.

51

Which choice provides the best evidence for the answer to the previous question?

A) Lines 60–63 ("Some... pristine")

B) Lines 74–76 ("The resources... Earth")

C) Lines 81–83 ("One... avoided")

D) Lines 85–87 ("Without... insecure")

52

Which point about the resources that will be highly valued in space is implicit in Passage 1 and explicit in Passage 2?

A) They may be different resources from those that are valuable on Earth.

B) They will be valuable only if they can be harvested cheaply.

C) They are likely to be primarily precious metals and rare earth elements.

D) They may increase in value as those same resources become rare on Earth.

★ 真经派精讲

Question 42

In lines 9–17, the author of Passage 1 mentions several companies primarily to?

A) note the technological advances that make space mining possible.

B) provide evidence of the growing interest in space mining.

C) emphasize the large profits to be made from space mining.

D) highlight the diverse ways to carry out space mining operations.

1. 答案

B) 为对太空采矿增长的兴趣提供证据。

2. 精讲

分析目的题。

原文第 9–17 行给出了几个大写专有名词代表的公司或组织的表态。这种罗列几个例子的写作手法，必然是为了证明作者的某一观点。而这一观点很有可能在举例之前的中心句中，即第三段首句：The forum comes hot on the heels of（紧跟着）the 2012…

注意到该中心句里的核心词 hot（火爆，热闹）。这个 forum（论坛）有多 hot 呢？于是作者在接下来就用例证的写法，列举了几个公司的表态，它们正在做什么。所以，原文第 9–17 行的写作目的就是证明这个 forum 很 hot。那么这个 forum 是关于什么的呢？第一段讲了：mining beyond Earth。

所以，B 选项中 growing interest 对应原文 comes hot；space mining 对应 mining beyond Earth。

如果我们只用一个单词来总结第三段的中心思想，这个单词就是 hot。理解了这一

点，选项 A、C、D 自然轻松排除。

复习：要分析句子的写作目的，重点要考查自然段内的句间逻辑关系：哪一句是中心，哪一句是解释，哪一句是例证等。搞懂句子间的逻辑，那么某句话的写作目的和功能就清晰了。

Question 43

The author of Passage 1 indicates that space mining could have which positive effect?

A) It could yield materials important to Earth's economy.

B) It could raise the value of some precious metals on Earth.

C) It could create unanticipated technological innovations.

D) It could change scientists' understanding of space resources.

---

1. 答案

A) 它可能出产对地球经济来说很重要的物资。

Question 44

Which choice provides the best evidence for the answer to the previous question?

A) Lines 18–22 ("Within... lanthanum")

B) Lines 24–28 ("They... projects")

C) Lines 29–30 ("In this... commodity")

D) Lines 41–44 ("Companies... machinery")

---

1. 答案

A)

2. 精讲

较简单的细读题和引证题组合。

先定位第 33 题题干，回原文寻找太空采矿的 positive effect。

阅读到第 19 行，meeting earthly demands（满足地球上的需求），这个表达其实就是太空采矿的一个 positive effect。

那么地球上需求什么呢？后面说 demands for precious metals, such as platinum and gold, and the rare earth elements vital for personal electronics…

注意到 metals 和 the rare earth elements（稀土元素）对应 A 选项中的 materials（物资）。

文章中的 precious（珍贵的）和 vital（重要的）对应 A 选项中的 important。

句子中其他单词看不懂，但 gold（黄金）和 personal electronics（个人电子设备）对应 A 选项中的 Earth's economy（地球经济），这个同义归纳替换相信大家是可以理解的。

A 选项中的 yield（产生）一词貌似原文没有对应，其实来自全文中心 space mining 中的 mining（采矿）。

你瞧，A 选项中的每一个单词都在原文中找到了对应，还想什么呢？选 A，其他三个选项根本不看。这就是一个高手做题的心理活动全程。

高手做题其实是在玩一个连连看的游戏，感受明察秋毫的快乐，很 enjoy。

第 44 题解析：高手做完第 43 题，顺手为本题选出 A 选项，然后轻蔑地笑了笑。

做题时间 1 秒；笑了笑，又费时 1 秒。

本题费时共 2 秒。

Question 45

As used in line 19, "demands" most nearly means

A) offers.

B) claims.

C) inquiries.

D) desires.

1. 答案

D) 渴望的事物。

2. 精讲

词义题。

回原文第 19 行，注意到常见搭配: meet demand（满足需求）。demand 在这里指"需求"，同义词为 want，desire。

干扰选项 offers（提议）、claims（申明）、inquiries（询问）可排除。

Question 46

What function does the discussion of water in lines 35–40 serve in Passage 1?

A) It continues an extended comparison that begins in the previous paragraph.

B) It provides an unexpected answer to a question raised in the previous paragraph.

C) It offers hypothetical examples supporting a claim made in the previous paragraph.

D) It examines possible outcomes of a proposal put forth in the previous paragraph.

1. 答案

C) 它提供了假想的例子去支持上一段的论点。

2. 精讲

题干中问 function（作用，功能），分析目的题。

注意到四个选项中都提到了 previous paragraph，显然不仅要阅读第 35–40 行，还要阅读上一个自然段，然后理解这两个自然段的逻辑关系。

先阅读第 29 行开始的自然段，该段中心很明确：水很重要。

下一自然段说，水除了 let you live 之外，还能（could）用于干这个，还能（could）干那个。

显然，后一个自然段是例证，证明前一个自然段的观点。

因此，选出 C 选项。注意 C 选项中 hypothetical（假设的，设想的）一词对应原文中的两个 could。

干扰选项 A 和 B 都有迷惑性。上一自然段确实提出了 question（问题），也出现了 comparison（对比），原文：沙漠中，黄金重要还是水重要？随后原文马上给出一个意料之中的常识答案：当然水重要。

在接下来的自然段中，没有 continues an extended comparison（继续对比），所以 A 选项错；也没有提供 an unexpected answer（一个意料之外的答案），所以 B 错。

D 选项中说上一自然段提出一个 proposal（提议），原文没有，原文只是一个 claim：水重要。

Question 47

The central claim of Passage 2 is that space mining has positive potential but

A) it will end up encouraging humanity's reckless treatment of the environment.

B) its effects should be thoughtfully considered before it becomes a reality.

C) such potential may not include replenishing key resources that are disappearing on Earth.

D) experts disagree about the commercial viability of the discoveries it could yield.

1. 答案

B) 在成为现实之前，它的影响应该被全面考虑。

2. 精讲

分析论点题。

凡是涉及全文中心观点的题，我们都建议先空出，先做后面的题目。这样在做完后面的细节题后，大家会对全文加深理解，便于选择中心思想。

当然，如果你是真经派超级高手，也可以直接选出 B 选项。

超级高手的做题思路如下：

第 47 题题干中 space mining has positive potential 这个表达是对第一自然段的总结；题干中 but 一词对应第二段第一个单词 but；第二段 but 后的句子是全文中心句：we should pause to thought；后面的文章内容多次提及 careful consideration 和 consider。

这些都统统对应 B 选项中 thoughtfully considered。

这就是超级高手的快速解题过程。

以上思路只供欣赏，不可轻易模仿，否则后果自负。

一般人解题流程请参考后面第 49 题解析。

Question 48

As used in line 68, "hold" most nearly means

A) maintain.

B) grip.

C) restrain.

D) withstand.

---

1. 答案

A) 维持。

2. 精讲

词义题。

先理解原文该句中 those 指代上一个自然段的观点，尤其指代上一自然段中首句 principles 一词。

然后，通过上下文，可以理解出 hold 一词所在句子的表达：历史表明，这些原则将是我们应该 hold 的底线。

所以，hold 一词在文中对应的中文含义应该是"坚守，坚持，维持，维护"。

选出 A 选项 maintain（维持，维护）。

干扰选项 B) grip（抓住，紧握）；C) restrain（控制，抑制）；D) withstand（承受）。

Question 49

Which statement best describes the relationship between the passages?

A) Passage 2 refutes the central claim advanced in Passage 1.

B) Passage 2 illustrates the phenomenon described in more general terms in Passage 1.

C) Passage 2 argues against the practicality of the proposals put forth in Passage 1.

D) Passage 2 expresses reservations about developments discussed in Passage 1.

1. 答案

D) 第二篇短文对第一篇短文中讨论的发展表达了保留意见。

2. 精讲

理解两篇短文的关系，属于综合题中的分析多文本题。

其实本题和前面的第 47 题考点相似，都要理解第二篇短文的中心思想。所以，大概率是：第 47 题和第 49 题都对，或这两题都错。"贵粉儿"请先自己看看。

第一篇短文的中心大家通过阅读和前面的解题已经比较清楚了，讲到：太空采矿越来越 hot，会带来 positive effects。

第二篇短文第一自然段承接上文，第二段启下，第二段首句 But 强转折后，出现第二篇短文的全文中心句：we should pause for thought（我们应该停下来思考）。就是给第一篇短文中的 hot 泼泼凉水，让大家不要头脑太发热。

接下来第 59 行出现 careful consideration；第 74 行出现 consider；最后一段讲，大家应该先就一些 questions 达成 consensus（共识）和 agreement（一致）。

所以，第二篇短文不是全盘否定（refute，against）太空采矿，而是说呼吁深思熟虑，不要太冒进，应该提前就一些问题进行讨论达成一致。

D 选项中的 expresses reservations（表达了保留意见）十分贴切。

本题做完后，大家可以跳回第 47 题，轻松选出 B 选项。第 47 题 B 选项中的 thoughtfully consideration 是关键词，其实也是 reservations 的同义表达。

Question 50

The author of Passage 2 would most likely respond to the discussion of the future of space mining in lines 18–28, Passage 1, by claiming that such a future

A) is inconsistent with the sustainable use of space resources.

B) will be difficult to bring about in the absence of regulations.

C) cannot be attained without technologies that do not yet exist.

D) seems certain to affect Earth's economy in a negative way.

1. 答案

B) 在缺乏管控的情况下，会比较难实现。

Question 51

Which choice provides the best evidence for the answer to the previous question?

A) Lines 60–63 ("Some... pristine")

B) Lines 74–76 ("The resources... Earth")

C) Lines 81–83 ("One... avoided")

D) Lines 85–87 ("Without... insecure")

1. 答案

D)

2. 精讲

分析多文本题和引证题组合。

第 50 题题干比较长，先阅读题干指示的第一篇短文的第 18–28 行，发现该段中心讲太空采矿可以满足地球对稀有金属物资的需求，做出经济上的贡献。而且前面第 43 题也已经考查过，重点理解过。

第 50 题题干问在第二篇短文中作者如何回应这一观点。在解题时，如果你对第二篇文章印象深刻，中心理解到位，可直接定位到末段。反之，则可利用后面第 51 题四个选项去寻证阅读。

第二篇短文中，作者承认太空采矿的经济收获，但强调要深思熟虑，谋定而后动。第 85 行说，如果就一些问题不能达成一致，那么投资就会风险高，回报就会不安全（investments risky, and the gains made insecure）。

第 50 题 B 选项中的 absence 一词对应原文末段的 avoided 和 without；regulations 对应末段的 regulation，agreement 和 consensus。

第 51 题相应选出 D 选项。

Question 52

Which point about the resources that will be highly valued in space is implicit in Passage 1 and explicit in Passage 2?

A) They may be different resources from those that are valuable on Earth.

B) They will be valuable only if they can be harvested cheaply.

C) They are likely to be primarily precious metals and rare earth elements.

D) They may increase in value as those same resources become rare on Earth.

1. 答案

A) 它们可能和在地球上价值高的资源是不一样的。

2. 精讲

分析多文本题。

读懂读清楚题干之后，本题就不难了。

题目问：关于在太空中很有价值的资源，下面哪个观点是在短文 1 中暗示而在短文 2 中明示的？

还记得短文 1 中关于水的描述吗？文中用 in the desert（在沙漠中）这个场景类比，表明了在太空中也一样，水比黄金更珍贵；暗示了在地球和太空，在不同的环境和情况下，同一种资源价值不同。

在短文 2 中第 74 行，这个暗示被直接写出来了：The resources (that are valuable in orbit and beyond) may be very different to those (we prize on Earth). 注意括号中是两个定语从句。

所以选出 A 选项。

选其他三个干扰选项的考生，很大可能是没有认真读懂题目，无法定位原文出处，只能通过所谓的直觉，其实是"幻觉"，来选择。

⭐ 参考译文

第一篇短文改编自 2013 年《新科学家》杂志中 Michael Slezak 的文章《太空采矿：下一个淘金潮？》。第二篇短文来自该杂志主编同年的文章《驯服最后的边界》。

Passage 1

跟着钱，最后你会进入太空。这个信息来自一个第一次召开的有关地外采矿课题的论坛。

由澳大利亚太空工程研究中心召集的在悉尼召开的此次会议云集了采矿公司、机器人专家、月球科学家和政府机构，他们正在一起努力将太空采矿变为现实。

在 2012 年两家私营的小行星采矿公司刚刚成立后，这个论坛随之变得炙手可热。华盛顿行星资源公司表示，在未来的两年它将启动它的第一个望远镜，弗吉尼亚深太空工业公司希望到 2020 年能够去小行星上开采金属。另外一个出现在 2012 年的商业企业，科罗拉多州的金钉公司（Golden Spike）将为人们提供去月球的旅行，这其中包括潜在的月球采矿者。

在未来的几十年中，这些公司有可能会满足人们对贵金属的需求，比如铂金、黄金和对于个人电子设备极其重要的地球稀有元素，如钇和镧。但是，正如那些在美国的淘金潮中改变了美国西部的淘金者一样，这些最早的太空采矿者也并不只是能使他们自己富有，他们也希望建立一种脱离地球的经济，而这种经济将会与地球没有任何的联系。在这种经济中，从月球或小行星中提取和加工出来的材料被运输用于各种太空项目。

在这种情况下，从太空中采集的水可能会变成人们最想得到的商品。来自纽约蜜蜂机器人公司的 Kris Zany 问道："在沙漠里，哪一个更珍贵：一公斤黄金还是一公斤水呢？"他说："黄金是没有用的，而水会让你活下来。"

来自月球极地的冰可以被送到国际太空站供宇航员饮用或者用作抗辐射的盾。把水分解成氧和氢可以给航天飞船提供燃料，因此富含冰的小行星可以成为行星之间的燃料补给站。

许多公司正在把目标锁定在月球土壤里和小行星上的铁、硅、铝，这些原材料可以被用于 3D 打印来制造零件或机器。其他的公司想将太空中的灰尘变成混凝土，用于制造登陆站、住宅和道路。

Passage 2

　　进行太空旅行的原动力正在由纯粹的探索转变成经济利益。在去年，人们提出了大量关于将太空中的财富带到地球的提议。毋庸置疑的是，这将产生许多亿万富翁，甚至更富有者。但我们所有人都将会受益：那些从太空中获得的矿产财富及其带动的各项新技术会给我们所有人带来好处。

　　但是，在那些采矿者发射他们的太空火箭之前，我们应该停下来好好地思考一番。乍一看，太空采矿似乎绕开了最关键的环境问题：在小行星上是没有（或许没有！）生命存在的，因此不存在破坏栖息地的问题。但是它带来的后果，不论是对地球还是对太空，都值得我们深思熟虑。

　　这种思考部分是关于原则的。有些人可能会觉得浩瀚荒芜的太空不应该是我们人类掠夺的对象，正如他们坚持认为地球的南北极应该保持原生态一样。而另一些人会提出：染指太空并不是人类更好地进行可持续发展的地球生活的一种可以接受的替代方式。

　　历史表明：这些原则是我们难以坚守的底线，而且我们确实很难让公众相信如此荒芜的环境是值得我们加以保护的。毕竟，它们太浩瀚了。比起穿越南极洲的冰原，有机会去体验太空的人少之又少。

　　我们还要考虑人们提出的所谓的"地球之外的经济"。地球之外的资源和那些我们珍视的地球上的资源有可能完全不同。说得委婉一些，关于这些资源的监管权问题人们只是刚刚谈起——而且相关的法律和规范都是碎片化的。

　　和地球上的采矿公司一样，进行太空探索的公司经常不愿意提及这些问题。上周在澳大利亚悉尼召开的太空采矿论坛上，十位发言人恳请免于对太空探索的监管。但是，如果这些公司在营利性的太空探索问题上可以达成广泛一致，它们其实才会得到更大的好处。如果缺少共识，它们的观点将会备受争议，投资就会有风险，回报就会变得不确定。达成共识才是我们长期的利益所在。

图书在版编目 (CIP) 数据

SAT阅读真经总纲 / 刘洪波编著.—北京：中国人民大学出版社，2020.6
ISBN 978-7-300-28099-8

Ⅰ. ①S… Ⅱ. ①刘… Ⅲ. ①英语-阅读教学-高等学校-入学考试-美国-自学参考资料
Ⅳ. ①H319.37

中国版本图书馆CIP数据核字（2020）第071302号

- 本书中所有理论、概念均系作者原创，如果引用需注明出处。
- 本书著作权归作者所有，版权归中国人民大学出版社，任何复印、引用均需征求著作权人及版权持有人同时同意。

SAT阅读真经总纲

刘洪波　编著
SAT Yuedu Zhenjing Zonggang

出版发行	中国人民大学出版社	
社　　址	北京中关村大街31号	**邮政编码**　100080
电　　话	010-62511242（总编室）	010-62511770（质管部）
	010-82501766（邮购部）	010-62514148（门市部）
	010-62515195（发行公司）	010-62515275（盗版举报）
网　　址	http://www.crup.com.cn	
	http://www.1kao.com.cn（中国1考网）	
经　　销	新华书店	
印　　刷	北京玺诚印务有限公司	
规　　格	170mm×230mm　16开本	**版　　次**　2020年6月第1版
印　　张	9　插页1	**印　　次**　2020年6月第1次印刷
字　　数	100 000	**定　　价**　29.80元

封面无防伪标均为盗版

版权所有　　侵权必究　　印装差错　　负责调换

GUIXUE.COM 学为贵

内部免费资料
配套音频练习
每日名师公益直播课

托福真经词汇
基础词汇,五维逻辑词群记忆法,轻松记单词
提分词汇,精选托福高频必考词,提分更高效

定制计划
一对一全方位诊断学员情况
分科制定完整备考计划

精品课程
解决词汇、语法、发音及
听说读写提分难题
名师大咖授课
查漏补缺,每日必备

托福会员
七大特权
托福备考一站式服务

北美留学
加拿大、美国高端留学
帮你上更好的北美名校

GUIXUE.COM
学为贵

学为贵托福真经课程

托福系统课

课程名称	托福入门	预备技能	基础词场景词考点词	基础语法核心语法长难句语法	听说并进读写互通	技巧课	托福密卷	模测模考	教材讲义
托福零起点预备班	✔	✔	✔	✔				2次	《GREAT国际英语》《GREAT国际英语（练习册）》
托福基础冲60分班			✔	✔	✔			2次	《托福词汇真经》《托福语法真经》《托福听力真经（基础段）》
托福强化冲90分班			✔	✔		✔	✔	2次	《托福听力真经总纲》《托福阅读真经总纲》《托福写作真经总纲》《托福口语真经总纲》《托福长难句真经》《托福听力真经（强化段）》
托福进阶冲100分班			✔	✔		✔	✔	2次	《托福听力真经总纲》《托福阅读真经总纲》《托福写作真经总纲》《托福口语真经总纲》《托福长难句真经》《托福听力真经（冲刺段）》

托福能力提升课

课程名称	课程内容	课程亮点
托福提分词汇班	听力场景词 阅读同替词 口语地道词 写作高分词	托福高频必考词轻松学 五维逻辑词群高效记忆
托福全科考前预测班	托福密卷考前预测 独家题库横扫考场	
托福长难句打卡集训营	5种句式 9个成分 3类词性 从简单到复杂，短期集训全掌握	
托福写作题库打卡集训营	考试高分范文 写作行文逻辑 独家高分素材 避免考试雷同	名师大咖授课 社群督学陪练 托福密卷私享
托福口语题库打卡集训营	通用故事集 通用理由集 独家独立口语通用素材库 选题全，分类精，预测准	
托福刷题营	实时更新托福密卷 托福真经备考体系 真经派托福备考技巧	

学为贵SAT真经课程
SAT冲1500+在线班

GMAT真经课程
GMAT冲700+在线班

最新最全托福资料
每天免费听力大咖陪练
名师1V1指导托福备考
欢迎扫码，一键领取